Pelican Books
Sabotage in Industry

Pierre Dubois is a French sociologist
working for the Centre Nationale
de la Recherche Scientifique. He is at
present researching into labour
relations at the Université de Paris
VIIe.

Pierre Dubois

Sabotage in Industry

translated by Rosemary Sheed

Penguin Books

Penguin Books Ltd, Harmondsworth,
Middlesex, England
Penguin Books, 625 Madison Avenue,
New York, New York 10022, U.S.A.
Penguin Books Australia Ltd, Ringwood,
Victoria, Australia
Penguin Books Canada Ltd, 2801 John Street,
Markham, Ontario, Canada L3R 1B4
Penguin Books (N.Z.) Ltd, 182-190 Wairau Road,
Auckland 10, New Zealand

Le Sabotage dans l'industrie first published by
Calmann-Lévy 1976.
This translation first published by Penguin Books 1979

Made and printed in Great Britain by
C. Nicholls & Company Ltd
Set in Monotype Times

Contents

Publisher's Preface

Sections of *Sabotage in Industry* presuppose some knowledge of industrial-relations practices and labour history in France. A brief outline follows; readers in search of further information are recommended to consult *The Labour Movement in Europe* by Walter Kendall (Allen Lane, 1975).

French trade unions have never organized a majority of workers; currently there are in the region of 3 million trade unionists in France, out of a salaried working population of some $17\frac{1}{2}$ million. In the Renault plant at Boulogne-Billancourt, reputed to be a union stronghold, at most 20 per cent of the workers are unionized. Closed shops are illegal. In the recent past there have been up to 2 million foreign workers, many of whom are in the country on contract and for whom union membership is hazardous.

The trade union movement has throughout the twentieth century been divided on political grounds; there is no national body uniting trade unionists in the manner of the British TUC. At present there exist three major national confederations, each embracing a number of industrial or general unions (*syndicats*) which do not, however, possess the autonomy exercised by TUC-affiliated unions. In addition there are a number of independent unions, the largest of which are the teachers' union, the Fédération de l'Éducation Nationale (claiming 450,000 members in 1968) and the whitecollar Confédération Générale des Cadres (250,000). The main union formations mentioned in this book are:

CGT: Confédération Générale du Travail – General Confederation of Labour
CFDT: Confédération Française Démocratique du Travail – French Democratic Confederation of Labour
CFTC: Confédération Française des Travailleurs Chrétiens – French Confederation of Christian Workers
FO: Force Ouvrière – Workers' Force

The CGT is the largest confederation, with an estimated membership of 1·3 million. Since 1947 it has been firmly under the control of the Communist Party. In 1948 the anti-Communist minority split and founded the CGT-FO, known usually simply as FO, which now has a membership of roughly 500,000. The FEN left the CGT at the same time, but declined to join FO. An entirely separate movement, basing itself on Christian Social ideas, was the CFTC. This organization evolved away from explicit endorsement of Catholicism in the period after the Second World War, the majority voting to change its name to CFDT in 1964. The CFDT currently has roughly 700,000 members. A minority of the CFTC refused to accept the new orientation, splitting to form the CFTC (Maintenu), known usually simply as CFTC and now organizing perhaps 100,000 workers. Of a different order is the Confédération Française du Travail, a 'union' widely believed to be subsidized by Simca and Citroën and used, mainly in the car industry, to break strikes: in 1977 CFT members shot and killed Pierre Lemaître on a picket line in Rheims.

Nothing comparable to the British shop-stewards' system exists in France. Numerically weak, with a fluctuating membership, the various confederations vie with one another for the same constituencies. Above all, the unions do not have bargaining rights at factory level as in Britain: wage rates are determined by the government through the legal minimum wage and by negotiation at regional level with the employers' associations. Wage rates at company level are unilaterally determined by the employers, sometimes after consultation with works committees. At plant level representative structures were established as a result of legal enactments in 1936 and 1946. They are the following:

délégués du personnel: employees' representatives
comités d'entreprise: works committees.

The *délégués du personnel* are elected by all employees, not merely union members, in undertakings with more than ten employees (in theory: this provision is widely ignored). Their role is to present grievances 'related to the *application* of wage rates and other occupational classifications, of the Labour Code and of other laws and regulations for the protection of workers' health, safety and social insurance'. *Comités d'entreprise* are in theory elected in all establishments with more than fifty employees. Their function is to supervise company welfare schemes; the employer is also required to consult the *comité* on the economic policies of the company. In practice, however, *comités d'entreprise* often amount to little more than sports and canteen committees. Elections to the *comités d'entreprise* are conducted normally on the basis of lists put forward by the unions. *Délégués du personnel* and representatives on *comités d'entreprise* are entitled in law to spend a number of hours per month carrying out their functions. A similar provision has applied since 1968 to *délégués syndicanx* (union representatives) for the distribution of union literature and the collection of dues.

Translator's Note

I am indebted to Howard Davis and Paul Walton for their help in checking that I have translated the industrial and sociological terminology into the correct English equivalents.

ROSEMARY SHEED

Introduction

Tyres by the thousand. Fifteen thousand a day. Several hundred pass the quality controller in every eight-hour period, one every forty seconds. His job is to examine and test each one for faults: any tyre that is defective must be set aside. Suppose he doesn't do his job properly – what then? A faulty tyre, perhaps ten faulty tyres, go on their way among the sound ones. It is easy enough not to check: just a matter of doing nothing. So – is he letting them through just from carelessness? Hard to say. However, if too many poor-quality tyres are getting past the controller it may be decided to employ an overseer, whose job it is to double-check by further testing. The overseer thus checks up on the controller, and the controller checks up on the worker, and a vicious circle is established: the worker can afford to be careless over the quality of his work; there is someone else checking up on it afterwards, so the risk to the customer is slight. The controller can afford to be careless, too, since there is someone else checking up after him. A perfect example of the wrong way to deal with bad workmanship, this, for it simply guarantees a wider spread of carelessness. A proliferation of controllers and repair workers in a company may well be the first indication that sabotage is going on.

Loaves by the thousand. There is wastage: several hundred kilos of flour a day. The machine slices and packs a loaf every two seconds. The worker in charge of it regulates the width of the slices and the speed of the slicing according to the type of bread and the size of the loaf. If it is set incorrectly, then the machine will turn out dozens of unsaleable loaves. If something happens to go wrong when no one is watching, there can be a hailstorm of bread as slice upon slice falls to the floor. In a large industrial bakery, as in the tyre factory, carelessness, whether deliberate or otherwise, is responsible for significant wastage. Perhaps this large-scale wastage of raw materials is the second indication that sabotage is going on.

But just what do we mean by sabotage? It is normally understood to mean the destruction of premises, of machines or of manufactured products. The employer consequently suffers a loss of production – either because he no longer has a factory, or because his machines are useless, or because his product has gone up in smoke or been rendered unsaleable. But there are other things workers can do which contribute just as much to reducing a firm's output, and I think it makes sense to include them in our concept of sabotage. So our definition of sabotage will cover everything done by workers, individually or collectively, to the manufactured product or the machinery of production, that results in lowering the quantity or quality of production, whether temporarily or permanently.

But as well as worker sabotage, there can be management sabotage. We may go so far as to say that some factories are only kept going by the workers disregarding the instructions they are given for doing their jobs. It may seem paradoxical to start a book on workers' sabotage with this statement, but there is ample evidence that it is true. There *is* sabotage by management. To produce anything takes time; yet the real working time that starts when all the conditions are absolutely right can represent as little as a third of the total time spent at work. Almost all non-productive time can be blamed on the administration and how things are run, and in this sense it really is sabotage: errors in the conception and specification of the product, poor manufacturing methods, time wasted, machines out of use or out of order, workers taken from their normal role in the production process to be put on to other jobs, trying to make too many different products, changing models too often, poor planning, shortage of raw materials, plant not properly maintained, inadequate consideration of the siting of machinery, a failure to understand production patterns (Sartin, 1970). These are just some of the possible forms of management sabotage in industry.

But there are others. Workers are well aware of this kind of organized sabotage; they will say (as in one lorry assembly plant), 'It's chaos' (Bernoux, Motte and Saglio, 1973). The management believe their decisions to be completely rational, whereas the workers can see the irrationality in action: machines function more or less well – some standing idle for days on end – equipment is inadequate, supplies are ordered without regard to need, periods of intense activity alternate with periods of virtual inactivity, the burden of work is divided quite unfairly as between one position and another, further investment seems to be made quite arbitrarily and made without proper planning, wages are not related to productivity and promotion goes to the submissive rather than those who produce most. In other words, the workers recognize that the firm exists more to protect a power-system than to foster efficient production.

Nor does management sabotage stop there. Lock-outs can bring production to a halt against the wishes of the workers, strike situations are exacerbated, work is badly organized, raw materials are squandered, unnecessary machinery is bought, production capacity is under-used, the division of work among the various production units can be chaotic, both machinery and products become obsolescent at an increasing pace, and the workers' skills are wasted by continual repetitive work and fragmentation. All this sabotage · by management is undoubtedly far more significant than any sabotage by workers.

In the teeth of management sabotage, the workers manage to keep the factories running, producing the goods and bringing in the profits. The workers are the 'underground' of industrial efficiency, breaking the company's regulations to get the job done. This can be demonstrated in a great many ways, above all by the effect of 'working to rule'; this consists in carrying out every operation with scrupulous attention to every order emanating from the production department, the administration or the rule-book, and it rapidly brings production to a standstill. 'It's a good thing we're here to get the work done.'

Medical officers and ergonomics experts have constantly pointed out that between 50 and 80 per cent of all working behaviour departs from the official norms as laid down by work-organization departments. They have shown that even assembly work is not purely automatic: in electrical engineering the production target can only be achieved by the workers disregarding company regulations (Wisner *et al.*, 1972). A machinist will vary what she does to adapt to the demands of time-pressure, of accidents, of innovations, or simply to experiment: sometimes she reverses the order of her operations to make them easier to memorize and thus easier to carry out, sometimes she finds quicker ways of doing some parts of a job. As the day goes on she gradually changes her posture to keep up a steady rhythm of work, getting more and more tired as she does so. Her movements are not just automatic: she is thinking all the time how best to adapt them to changing circumstances. Even in the most repetitive jobs, then, workers are far from being robots: if the desired production level is to be achieved they have to show continual initiative for the benefit of their firm. Were they to rest content with obeying orders to the letter, their factory would grind to a halt.

But this initiative can also be used to sabotage the work – merely by a slight variation of movement. If workers want to make use of the concealed power that the employer has perforce to give them, they are faced with two possible strategies. They can stick precisely to the official regulations, in which case production will ultimately be paralysed: a sabotage strategy, in other words. Or, by short-circuiting the official regulations, they can enable production to function properly: an anti-sabotage strategy. If they do the first, they sabotage production but break no rules; if the second, they speed up production but risk getting into trouble.

When workers are sick of seeing their indispensable role in society being ignored, they rebel and refuse to go on playing the game. That rebellion may take the form of sabotage, which is the main subject of this book. Industrial action of this kind still happens – in fact there is more sabotage today than there was a few years ago. This fact alone seems to me to justify my publishing this study. I have drawn upon various sources for my information: I have used existing work on the subject, as well as referring to my own research – studies of strikes in France and in Europe, of types of action in the most modern factories, of workers' reactions to working conditions. I begin by giving the facts: that sabotage takes place, what we know of its history, what it has aimed to achieve and what it has achieved. I then try to interpret those facts: what have been the effects of the theories now current in the workers' movement? Who are the saboteurs? To what extent must management accept responsibility for provoking sabotage? Finally I analyse the 'remedies' for sabotage adopted by management: repression and/or the search for new policies.

1. The forms of sabotage that reduce production are various: destroying machines and products, arson, theft, all-out strikes when production is completely stopped, going slow, working to rule, working without enthusiasm, absenteeism, high labour turnover, avoidance of employment, refusal to work in production industries, starting work later and retiring earlier. We shall estimate the harm done to the economy by these various factors, and their incidence, now and in the past.

2. Sabotage may be seeking to achieve different goals: to satisfy some immediate claim, to set in motion political changes or a revolutionary movement, or merely to express opposition to management. Machine-breaking in the late nineteenth century was directed not just to saving jobs; it was a protest against a new organization of work, against the abolition of skilled jobs and against the appearance of poor-quality goods on the market. Machines can also be destroyed for political purposes, as in France during the Second World War.

This section analyses the aims and results of long strikes, general strikes, go-slows and absenteeism. Several different forms of sabotage can happen at once in the same place, in which case there will be a number of different aims. At the Lip works in France in 1973 there was a go-slow, watches were stolen, the workers carried on in the absence of the management, and there was an indefinite strike. The demands were that there be no redundancies, no closure and no loss of benefits already acquired. In addition to these explicit demands, the workers were also contesting the absolute authority of the management and their divine right to dismiss people; they wanted the government to lose face; they wanted legal reforms; they wanted to strengthen the workers' movement, to indicate the possibility of other forms of work organization and to demonstrate the positive value of leisure.

3. It is in reference to these aims and results that the theory of the trade union movement is defined. In France there are two opposing tendencies in the workers' movement: the Marxist tradition and the anarchist tradition. The Marxist tradition, because it gives priority to gaining political power, rejects sabotage, the primary form of rebellion against management. The anarchist tradition justifies the use of sabotage as part of the day-to-day struggle to achieve immediate change. At the beginning of the century, the CGT was anarcho-syndicalist, and its congresses passed motions in favour of using sabotage in the context of a general revolutionary strike, or as a protest against national mobilization in case of war. After the First World War the supporters of sabotage were in the minority: the CGT remained hostile to it, except during the Second World War, allowing only of certain limited forms, such as the indefinite strike and the go-slow. In recent years the CFDT has unhesitatingly supported strikers who would not promise to ensure safety services. Some French Maoists today have returned to the pro-sabotage anarchist position.

4. Who are the saboteurs then, in situations when the trade unions are officially against the use of sabotage? Some maintain that sabotage originates among non-union workers – the unskilled who work in firms recently set up in areas where there has hitherto been no industry, young people, women, immigrants, in general workers with no industrial traditions. Others believe that it is a grassroots movement overflowing the bounds of bureaucratic organization, in which local union groups combine together. Yet others stress the key position of saboteurs in the production process: they must always work in a sensitive spot where it takes only a slight incident to cause major disruption. There is some truth in all these views; but it seems to me that sabotage always occurs at a specific moment in the history of the struggle inside each company, not just as the starting point of that history. A collective go-slow, for instance, only takes place where there has

been considerable previous experience of different forms of struggle.

5. Sometimes the responsibility for sabotage starting lies with the management: work organization, rates and methods of pay, working conditions, the pattern of authority, a refusal to recognize union organizations, management attitudes during strikes – all these may be a direct incitement to sabotage. When confronted with sabotage, a management can choose between two courses: repression or reform. Repression may be violent, disciplinary (dismissal of the saboteur) or penal (fines and/or imprisonment). Reform involves working out a new policy towards the workforce, aimed at getting rid of the causes of sabotage or the situations in which it occurs. Two solutions would seem to be the most effective: a complete reorganization of the work process, to the point of giving total responsibility for production to autonomous groups; and accepting the formalization of industrial conflict – that is to say recognizing the place of the unions in industry and setting up a permanent system of negotiating. Finally, employers also wage an ideological battle based on the myth of growth as the indispensable condition for social progress. Yet all these solutions, however up-to-date, will always be insufficient.

What the employers have to do then, if they are not already doing so, is to make the best of a bad job. Their companies will have to live with the problem of sabotage, not necessarily on a large scale, but regular and perhaps increasing. The remedies they will apply, and are already applying, can never do more than alleviate it. The only effective strategy therefore seems to be to assess the cost of sabotage along with the other outgoings of the firm, and plan to allow for it.

The trade unions too, if they are not already doing so, must make the best of a bad job. Sabotage is not going to disappear today just because they fulminate against it in an electoral campaign. The reasons for carrying on and indeed extending it are too compelling. The only effective strategy seems to be to pass over it in silence, thus stopping it from spreading more rapidly. Social change in the future, the establishment of a socialist system, would be a far more effective remedy for sabotage than any of the solutions now being tried by management. It remains extremely unlikely that we shall see all forms of sabotage disappear unless we know the answer to one vital question: would there be acts of sabotage if the workers did not feel like aliens in their factory, not owning the means of production, having no control over the process of manufacturing or even over the organization of their own work? How would it be if they had a right to be heard, a right to take part in formulating change?

So, revolutionaries too, if they are not already doing so, must make the best of a bad job. The time is past when people thought sabotage could be seen as one among other forms of revolutionary action to take political power, to gain control of the state. Today there are few saboteurs, and still fewer with any global political vision. Those there are, are mainly seeking satisfaction of immediate demands which may only incidentally have a political content.

On examination, it would seem that using some forms of sabotage to back up their demands can be an effective strategy for gaining limited changes in the workers' situation – in wages, and above all in improved working conditions. Of course the result achieved depends on a whole series of factors: the context, the current balance of forces, the possibilities of repression, the novelty of the form of action used, and so on. But it is this relative effectiveness, certainly equal to that of other more legally accepted methods, which must surely explain the growing volume of sabotage in the struggle for workers' rights today.

1 The Spread of Sabotage

'Workers' sabotage? That's all past history! A hundred years ago, yes, they broke machines, with angry shouts that mechanization was taking away their jobs and their livelihood. But workers today are disciplined: they have won social benefits and they have unions to defend them; negotiating structures work well, and no one would dream of damaging the tools of his trade.' Ten years ago it would have been true to say all this – there was just such a contrast between past and present. But today it is so no longer; workers' sabotage has returned.

We may distinguish three types of workers' sabotage: those where the object is to destroy machinery or goods (arson, direct damage to machines, refusal to operate safety services, vandalism, theft); those which stop production (strikes and various other ways of blocking production without actually destroying anything); and those which reduce the amount of work done (going slow, cutting down on working time, working to rule, working without enthusiasm, absenteeism, labour turnover and simply refusing to go into industry at all). This is a convenient distinction for the purposes of this introductory chapter, for it allows of an analytical presentation of the various methods used, which I shall illustrate with a number of examples both past and present. There are certain questions that inevitably spring to mind even at this early stage. Is sabotage a frequent occurrence? Can one estimate the damage done by it? Is there more or less today than in the past, and have methods changed? Following this first classification, we shall go on to consider others which lead into other forms of analysis: active and passive sabotage, offensive and defensive sabotage, individual and collective sabotage, open and covert sabotage, spontaneous and organized sabotage.

The destruction of machinery and/or goods

It may seem arbitrary to make a distinction between these two types of destructive sabotage, especially since in practice they are so often the same: arson destroys both machines and goods; a damaged implement damages the product it turns out. However, it is not just an academic distinction, for it is based on a distinction between the machine and the product that is traditional in the workers' movement. Why destroy machines which might well belong in future to those who operate them? Goods once sold, on the other hand, are out of reach once and for all – and at the time of manufacture the surplus-value concealed in them is not visible to the naked eye.

What are our sources for a study of destructive sabotage? Crime statistics only tell part of the story, for two reasons: first, the culprits may never be known, and second, the employers do not always prosecute. So one is obliged to make a special study of the problem itself (being careful to discount what we may call false sabotage, that is, accidental damage which is then transformed into an intentional act). One can, finally, find an indirect source in the statistics compiled by companies for other reasons (the amount of time machinery is in use, records of quality, reprimands for defective work, the size of the workshops where repairs and re-touching are done).

Arson

If it succeeds in its aims, or even goes beyond them, arson is indiscriminate: buildings, machinery and goods are all swept away. Explosives can have the same effect. In Great Britain from 1799 to 1824, when trade unions were illegal, industrial action took the most violent forms: small craft shops and large factories alike were burned down (Frow, Frow and Katanka, 1971). In 1820 the weavers' union in Glasgow, which had been unusually effectively organized since 1818, made all its members swear to implement any decision taken by the majority. Whenever there was a strike, a secret committee was set up, which the rest of the members knew nothing about and which put a price on the head of 'knobsticks and obnoxious manufacturers', and offered rewards for firing factories. One mill was destroyed in that way because women were employed there as strike-breakers (Engels, 1845). In September 1843

a similar attempt was made in Ibbetson's knife and file works ... Mr Ibbetson had made himself obnoxious by ... the exclusive employment of knobsticks, and the exploitation of the Poor Law for his own benefit ... Considerable damage was inflicted by the explosion, and all the working-men who came to view it regretted only 'that the whole concern was not blown into the air' [Engels, 1845].

A hundred years later, during the Second World War, there were several incidents of arson at the Renault works on the Île Séguin and their evacuated works at Belfort (R. Durand, 1971). Again since 1970 there have been cases of arson, when all or part of a factory has been destroyed: the Sonolor works at La Courneuve was largely destriyed in the night of 28 February – 1 March 1974; the warehouses of a large household electrical equipment manufacturer in Burgundy were burnt down early in 1972. There have been other, more limited incidents: in the France–Dunkerque yards in 1970, and in one of the Boussac factories in Lille in 1971.

Fire may not be recognized as sabotage, if those responsible do not admit their responsibility or if they are not found out. But it ca 1 often be to people's advantage to transform a fire that began accidentally into sabotage. The fact that a fire begins simultaneously in several different places is not absolute proof of sabotage, that is to say of *workers'* sabotage – for one must not ignore the usefulness of making a clean sweep of old-fashioned factories or superfluous stocks in times of economic difficulty. Arson by the proprietors cannot be ruled out *a priori*. Nor can arson by someone totally unconnected with the firm concerned. Criminal arson by persons unknown is, for the purposes of this study, a form of sabotage.

Machine-breaking

This can take various forms, but all tend to paralyse production. Luddism was a workers' movement in England whose high point was in 1811–12. During that period over 1,000 mills were destroyed by groups of organized and armed workers, some of them as large as 1,000 men.

The main disturbance commenced in Nottingham, in March 1811. A large demonstration of stockingers, 'clamouring for work and a more liberal price', was dispersed by the military. That night sixty stocking-frames were broken at the large village of Arnold by rioters who took no precautions to disguise themselves and who were cheered on by the crowd. For several weeks disturbances continued, mainly at night, throughout the hosiery villages of north-west Nottinghamshire. Although special constables and troops patrolled the villages, no arrests could be made [Thompson, 1963].

For the first two thirds of the last century machine-breaking continued sporadically in England. There was, for instance, the following incident in May 1843:

Pauling & Henfrey, a brick firm, had increased the size of the bricks without raising wages, and sold the bricks, of course, at a higher price ... the Brickmakers' Union declared war upon the firm ... When intimidation [against the knobsticks who were brought in] proved unavailing, the brick-yard, which lay scarcely a hundred paces from an infantry barracks, was stormed at ten o'clock one night by a crowd of brickmakers, who advanced in military order, the first ranks armed with guns. They forced their way in, fired upon the watchmen as soon as they saw them, stamped out the wet bricks spread out to dry, tore down the piled-up rows of those already dry, demolished everything which came in their way ...

Many of them were badly wounded and they were forced to withdraw, but 'the object of the visit – the demolition of all the destructible objects in the yard – was attained' (Engels, 1845).

Machine-breaking, in the sense of destroying machines simply as such, also occurred in France, though never as widely as in England: there was the breaking of the great cutting machine at Vienne in 1819, when the master-cutters and workers formed an alliance against two manufacturers who had decided to introduce a mechanical cutter into their factory. Machines were broken in 1833 during the strike of the 5,000 workers of the Anzin mining company. One of the last such incidents in France was in 1875, at the Fumay slate-works, where a mechanical saw introduced the previous year was badly damaged.

But damage to machines is not always part of a campaign against the machine as such, as the enemy of the worker's livelihood. There are other reasons, most commonly resulting from the workers' wish to halt production, during a strike for example. From this point of view, what matters above all is to sabotage a machine at a key point in the production process. We first find this kind of selective destruction in the mines, in the Loire valley strike of 1869: the valves of the boilers were broken, and the miners threatened to cut the cables of the lifts. No one could go down the mine shaft at all. As production systems became more complex, such selective sabotage naturally became more extensive. In 1885 the workers in the Rogelet combing factory removed the belts linking the machines with the source of power, so that they could no longer run. In 1890 the sugar workers of Étricourt in the Somme demolished the railway-lines along which the beet had to travel to the refinery (Perrot, 1973).

Selective sabotage also takes place today: it always involves more than just immediate damage to the machinery itself. When computers, power stations, telephone lines, radio and television transmitters or water supplies are sabotaged, it causes extended disruption.

Furthermore, there is no need to destroy machinery completely in order to stop it from working: just as the sabotaging of one key machine can cause general disruption, so the sabotaging of one key component of a machine can cause it to come to a standstill. In 1888 the glovemakers in the Perrin workshop at Grenoble broke the needles of their sewing machines, thus rendering them temporarily useless (Perrot, 1973). In 1895, the railwaymen's union threatened to use sabotage to stop the passage of a law intended to make trade unions illegal: 'With two small coins of the right shape used judiciously we can completely prevent a locomotive from running' (Pouget, 1910). In 1970 the electrical fittings of several cranes were disconnected in the France-Dunkerque yards (Faye, 1973). In 1971 iron bars were inserted into the lines in the Brandt works in Lyon, causing them to stop instantly.

Other forms of sabotage against machines are rather more

sophisticated, in as much as it is not possible to prove that the damage done is intentional. Back at the turn of the century, F. W. Taylor described how some workers who wanted to show the management that their scientific methods of work organization were both absurd and dangerous, purposely ran their machines as hard as possible until they broke down; the only reason that he knew it was sabotage was that he was employed as a worker there himself. There are some quite recent instances of a similar kind. A steelworker let too cold a slab go into the rolls, with the result that the steel had to be recycled and the rolls were ruined (Taylor and Walton, 1971). In another steelworks, the rollers did something equally risky: to reduce the number of cuts, they tightened the screws of the cylinders a little more than was called for, with the result that sometimes the cylinders cracked. Was it sabotage? Well, it was not intended as such, but in its foreseeable consequences, it was. In the steel industry today over three quarters of all machine-failures are never found to be imputable to anyone: are they due to the material, to a fault in the machine, or to an error, intentional or otherwise, on the part of the operator? No one knows for sure (C. Durand, Prestat and Willener, 1972). But there are those who have no hesitation in saying that a lot of accidents are not 'accidents' at all. Intentional mistakes are made in handling machinery or checking it; maintenance is left too late to stop it from breaking down.

Is the refusal to carry out safety precautions in highly integrated production units (such as iron, aluminium or paper) sabotage, or not? The workers in one of the Béghin paper-works went on strike at the end of 1970, and left it to the management to stop the machines. Were they saboteurs? In 1973 when the Pechiney-Noguères workers decided to abandon responsibility for the aluminium electrolysis tanks, and leave it to the managerial staff, were they saboteurs? In the first case, no harm was done; in the second, some of the tanks were out of action for several months because the aluminium in them had solidified. Is one to go by the intention or the result? In neither case did they set out directly to destroy the means of production, but they knew what the risks were: both were borderline sabotage. Slightly different was another borderline case in April 1975: the Usinor-Dunkerque steelworkers refused to let the mixers (into which the cast-iron flowed from the blast-furnaces) be emptied. The strikers claimed that there was no risk to the mixers at the point when the management called the police in to evacuate the premises. Would the workers have let the machinery of production be ruined if the police had not come? Probably not, but they went farther than in their 1971 strike, when they had done nothing to prevent the mixers being emptied.

A discussion of sabotaging machinery must, finally, include the loss or destruction of tools – a form of sabotage which can occur in non-mechanized work as well. For instance, some men whose job it was to clean out the tanks of a ship saved themselves extra work by smashing their buckets against a bulkhead. Since the foreman could not provide substitutes, he could only call a halt to the whole activity (Taylor and Walton, 1971).

Vandalizing the work premises (by breaking windows, for instance), the watchman's lodge at the factory gates, the homes of the employers, the office equipment, is only indirectly sabotage in our terms since it does not necessarily involve any diminution either of the quantity or quality of production.

Sabotage of the product

Several of the examples I have given involve damage simultaneously to machinery and goods. We now turn to direct sabotage of the manufactured product, when goods are destroyed, stolen, made totally or partially unusable, or the materials that go into them are wasted. This kind of thing is sabotage to the extent that it contributes to reducing production, whether quantitatively or qualitatively. Theft belongs in this class because it causes a certain proportion of the finished goods to disappear altogether.

Theft by workers is a longstanding custom. In 1830 we hear from an employer who could only explain it by his men's passion for gambling. He advised his colleagues to use stern measures:

Don't employ gamblers. A man who gambles is bound to lose in the end; then, naturally he wants to win his money back. But he can't play to win it back if he has nothing. So all he can do is steal, which he does. Furthermore a gambler is always thinking about his winnings and losses, he becomes obsessed by his unhappy passion, and so becomes apathetic and loses all interest in his work [Bergerie, 1829–30].

At the end of the last century, there was a lot of thieving during strikes – lengths of material were stolen and shared out among the strikers (Perrot, 1973). Nowadays many firms whose finished products are relatively small and in common use recognize that there is persistent thieving: household appliances, shoes, toilet articles and clothes vanish from factories or stores. Some firms will differentiate between theft for personal use and theft for re-sale, almost excusing the former. As one employer remarked, 'A factory is a real thieves' paradise. There's nothing they don't take. Pilfering goes on all the time' (quoted in Lourau, 1974).

Sometimes, when workers strike against mass lay-offs, they seize quantities of finished products. The Lip case in 1973 was outstanding: the workers took watches and sold them, and shared out the money they made as unofficial strike pay. When matters were settled early in 1974, all watches that had not been sold and monies not shared out were handed over to the new employers. No charges were ever preferred, but legally speaking it was undoubtedly theft. The Lip affair set an example: the Robin strikers sold trousers in 1973; in 1974 the Belgian Ampex strikers sold electrical equipment, and the Manuest strikers sold kitchen and bathroom furnishings; in 1975 the BSN Mécaniver strikers sold plate glass, the Everwear strikers bedspreads, the Teppaz strikers amplifiers and the Val Saint-Lambert strikers decorative glassware. And here is a slightly different case, when local farmworkers turned burglars to help some strikers: 'On 13 November 1974 a gang of twenty or thirty agricultural labourers unloaded a lorry belonging to the Négobeureuf company. The contents, consisting of twenty-two cases of camembert, 500 kilos of butter and several dozen pots of yoghurt, were taken to the workers in a firm in Pontivy who had been on strike for two weeks' (*Le Monde*, 21 February 1975).

Manufactured products can be made permanently unusable, either directly (by vandalism) or indirectly (for instance by holding up the transport of perishable goods). There was a historic instance of this in Ireland in 1880, when some tenants in County

Mayo decided to ostracize their landlord's agent, Captain Boycott, and would not allow his crops to be brought in. Whenever any transport strike becomes at all widespread or prolonged, there are likely to be consequences of this sort: in the big British dock strike of July 1970, the government declared a state of emergency and sent troops into the ports to unload perishable goods. In France, early in 1975, fishermen on strike decided to make their action more effective by holding up lorries bringing in foreign fish until the fish was uneatable.

Vandalism of products can take many forms: at the Eaux de Vittel company in 1970, soap was added to several tanks of water; tiny holes were also made in the plastic bottles, so that they were empty on reaching their destination. In another firm, a ton of toothpaste overflowed the processing machine and could not be used. Material can also be lost following a work stoppage: in May 1971 the workers in one of the Saint-Frères factories disconnected their machines several times a day, and each time the plastic solidified and was wasted. In the spring of 1975 vans transporting printed copies of the newpaper *Parisien libéré* out of the country were attacked and the papers destroyed. Stewards on ships have also been known deliberately to burn passengers' shirts when ironing them. It is also worth recalling the scandal uncovered in the Italian postal service in 1974: a backlog of tons and tons of mail, far too much to deliver, was pulped. That was a decision of the postal authorities, but the postal workers probably made a lot of letters disappear at an earlier stage.

More often, however, sabotaged goods can be saved: they are sold as seconds, or even sometimes touched up and sold as top quality goods. The Lyon silk-weavers used to cheat on weight. They had to give their employer the same weight of woven material as they had been given silk to weave (with a certain percentage allowed for wastage). When prices were bad the weavers would incorporate the weight of some foreign matter (water or oil) in the woven cloth, and so be able to keep back some of the raw silk for their own use. This practice was widespread after the failure of the insurrection of November 1831 (Moissonnier, 1975).*

*A demonstration of weavers in Lyon in October 1831 won the restoration of a minimum tariff for their work, lowered as a result of economic

At the turn of the century, the proof-readers' union, whose members had a high professional standing and were always expected to work conscientiously, had no hesitation in recommending sabotage when the employers broke the terms of their contract: misprints were then inserted purposely into the texts (Blondeau, 1973). There are a great many examples of this type of sabotage today: cuts made in lengths of cloth, sub-standard goods that the firm has to sell at a lower price, plastics mixed to produce objects not of the standard colour, joints badly soldered, equipment with faults in the electrical circuit, letters and telegrams delivered hundreds of kilometres away from the right address, telephone switchboards jammed for a period so that no lines are working. In the car industry there was sabotage at the Fiat works in 1968-9 and the Lordstown General Motors factory in the early 1970s: windscreens were broken, banana skins slipped into the fuel tanks, wings dented. And a fina rather comic example: to support a wage demand, some cinema technicians projected films upside-down or on the ceiling, introduced new and alarming sounds and mixed reels from different films (Taylor and Walton, 1971)

One last way of sabotaging products is wasting materials in terms of what is normally allowed for by the firm: a cook can serve larger helpings or use better materials; a secretary can put more stamps than necessary on the mail; a carpenter can put a thicker piece of wood into a cupboard than the specification allows for. This sort of thing, of course, can benefit the consumer. W. Mellor, writing in 1920, called for non-violent sabotage to demonstrate how poorly produced some commodities were, and urged workers to refuse to collaborate in such inferior articles. Building workers, in particular, could hardly want to be associated with jerry-built houses designed not to last. He found it surprising that the English unions had never recommended action of this kind.

---

depression. Within a short while the merchants repudiated this agreement, provoking a strike which the authorities tried to suppress by force. The weavers, together with a section of the National Guard, seized the city. They were crushed by royal troops, and the tariff of prices was revoked.

The spread of destructive sabotage: historical development

One has to exercise some caution, for the available sources are anything but homogeneous. Arson is infrequent, and so is the direct destruction of machinery and goods. Other forms of sabotage, more generalized, harder to spot or prove, should logically be more widespread; in fact they still remain the exception. The total loss of production caused in this way is negligible, except perhaps in the particular factory concerned. The form of sabotage that causes the greatest losses to industry is undoubtedly theft.

The theory that violent action in the workers' movement is on the decline, and that sabotage of machinery and goods is on the way out, is based on this apparent infrequency and the tiny numbers of people who seem to be involved. But little is known for certain. Of course we have not experienced the waves of machine-breaking found among the Luddites in early nineteenth-century England. But there have been spurts of sabotage more recently than that. In France during the last war acts of sabotage against the railways amounted to 171 in 1941, 276 in 1942 and many more in the years following: destroying electrical equipment, blocking lines, causing derailments by removing rails, cutting brake cables, throwing sand into the bearings, planting explosives beside lines, tunnels and points, destroying mechanical cranes and shovels, burning the wood used in the engines, and simply changing the labels on the trucks (Jacquet, 1967). Similarly, at the Renault works after the 1942 bombardment, acid was thrown into gear-boxes, emery powder into engines; one vital machine for tooling aeroplane motor parts was put completely out of commission, the electricity supply was cut, nuts were left loose, armoured cars were damaged, crank-shafts were hammered out of true, water-pumps chromium-plated defectively (R. Durand, 1971). The post office was sabotaged too. Special groups were formed to intercept the mail of the German services, to abstract letters of denunciation, to listen in to telephone conversations, cut them off or produce faults on the line making them inaudible, and to sabotage a number of radio stations. As the liberation began, the number of telephone and telegraph wires being cut rose sharply (Frischmann, 1967).

It seems, then, that we can characterize the present situation thus: waves of large-scale sabotage against a permanent, irreducible background of widespread but less evident sabotage. This latter is the sabotage of today. In addition to the examples I have given, a number of other phenomena imply the existence of small-scale sabotage: there would be no need, for example, for the proliferation of checking systems and repair services in factories if work was being properly done; the fact that the Taylorian system has been proposed in some factories is also surely significant. Another modern development is the shift from total destruction of machinery to partial destruction that has just as paralysing an effect.

If we study the sabotaging of machinery and goods during strikes (excluding what goes on when there is no strike) we find ourselves with rather more precise information, though not all the research that has been done is equally representative. In her exhaustive study of strikes in France from 1871 to 1890, M. Perrot finds that there was violence (i.e. collective and physical aggression against people or property) in 3·6 per cent of strikes, the annual rate ranging from 0·4 to 10 per cent; there is no marked trend either way over the period. She does not give figures relating specifically to violence against property, but from the series of examples she gives, violence would seem to have been fairly equally distributed as between animate and inanimate targets.

E. L. Shorter and C. Tilly, in their research into French strikes from 1890 to 1935 – based solely on press reports – give lower percentages than those given by Perrot for the preceding period. From 1890 to 1914 there was violence in 1·6 per cent of strikes, and from 1915 to 1935, in 0·2 per cent. However, they have a fairly restricted definition of violence: it must be the work of a group, and cause fairly wide damage to property.

In our own investigation of the strikes of 1968 (Dubois, Dulong and Durand, 1971) we only found a few cases of sabotage, and these were not strictly speaking destructive: certain manufactured goods were taken from stock and distributed without the employer's consent. The idea of selling or giving away goods was considered in a number of cases; at Lip it was actually put into effect. In 1968 there was overwhelming respect for tools and machinery, and all safety regulations were scrupulously observed. But 1968 was perhaps a peak point of non-sabotage in the history of the workers' movement. Certainly, in a later study of 123 strikes in 1971, we found seven cases of obvious sabotage either of goods or of machinery; but since our sample concentrated on the larger disputes, the proportion of sabotage over the whole range of strikes (there were over 4,500 in 1971) was probably considerably lower (Dubois and Durand, 1975).

What are we to learn from these comparisons? Are we to conclude that violent strikes and sabotage are on the decline, as the differences in the figures, though tiny, suggest? I think not. My own conclusion is that destructive sabotage is rare, and always has been, but it is not unknown; it has never totally vanished from the history of the workers' movement, and today, as in the past, it crops up here and there, on a greater or lesser scale. The fact that respect for the means of production prevails in the workers' movement should not blind us to the existence of a minority who have no such respect. And both attitudes need explaining. Destructive sabotage results in a lowering of production; but do the work stoppages and various forms of slowing down work that we find today have the same disruptive effects? In other words, are they really sabotage as well?

Stopping production

Is a strike sabotage? Does it result in both a quantitative and a qualitative drop in production? Every major strike – at least if it is of any length or in a key sector of the economy – invariably provokes some such statement from the government as this: 'The continuance of this strike/these strikes will result in damage to the economy.' In France, in the autumn of 1948, the miners were accused of getting involved in a vast, foreign-controlled conspiracy of sabotage and revolution. Similar stirring statements were made about the strikes in the public sector in 1953 and 1968 and in the post office at the end of 1974.

That strikers intend to disrupt production by stopping work seems to go without saying. But do they in fact succeed in their aim? To many people this is just a rhetorical question: those who see every strike as sabotage also believe that the right to strike should be restricted if not altogether denied. On the other hand, those who defend this traditional weapon of the workers' movement against attack tend to play down the extent of the economic disruption it causes.

Studies of the relationship between the development of industrial production and the frequency, scope and duration of strikes always consider the problem from the same viewpoint: they all examine the influence of the economic situation on strikes, and not the other way round. Why so?

It does not appear that variations in the number of strikes can be responsible for the variation in economic factors. But one is deflected somewhat from this question by the virtual unanimity of all the authors who have studied the problem: strikes have little direct effect on the country's economy . . . They change neither the movement of the wage index nor the development of the overall economic situation [Andréani, 1968].

The strike – which stops production – apparently results in no lowering of production. How can this paradox be?

There is one phenomenon that may mask the effect of strikes on the development of production: a number of writers (Perrot, Andréani, Goetz-Girey, Shorter and Tilly) have noted a positive (though not in fact very significant) link between economic growth and the increase of strikes – there are more strikes during a period of expansion. So perhaps the fall in production caused by strikes is masked by the general movement of expansion; it is not large enough to reverse the trend of expansion but only to slow down that expansion slightly. A more recent study (Scardigli, 1974) has provided further nuances: two contradictory hypotheses are both partially true. First, as I have just said, there is a positive correlation between production and strikes: when production shows marked growth, strikes are more numerous (the workers wanting a larger slice of the cake, and believing themselves to be in a strong position to get it). Secondly – contrary to that first hypothesis – there is an inverse correlation between production growth and strikes: when growth is marked, strikes go down (there is no need to strike against lay-offs, and employers yield more readily to demands). Both these hypotheses can be shown to be true, but over different periods. In other words, strikes increase in times of economic expansion; but for different reasons they may also increase in certain periods of economic recession. However, this analysis takes its conclusions no further; it does not, for instance, try to show whether, in a time of recession, strikes have the effect of worsening the real or relative fall in production. It merely says: 'In the first analysis, the total cost to the economy is not great, since strikes involve the loss of less than three hours' work per wage-earner per year, and the growth of our gross domestic product over a long period is no less than that of countries where there are ten or twenty times fewer strikes.'

The second phenomenon that can mask the effect of strikes on production growth results from the fact that it is always *annual* statistics that are used: it may well be that monthly variations within the year would be significant for our purpose. However, one must distinguish several different levels of analysis: a particular strike may (or may not) affect the production of the factory concerned, of the company that owns the factory, of that sector of economic activity or of industrial production as a whole. For instance, the twenty-four-day French miners' strike in 1963 ultimately caused a production loss of about 10 per cent. But there is a second type of situation when the production lost in a strike is partly or even wholly made up in later months. May–June 1968 is an excellent example of this change of tempo – a spectacular drop and then a sudden recovery. As compared with April, production fell by 31 per cent in May and 21 per cent in June (these figures are reduced if building and public works are included). The lost production began to be recovered in July, but from October onwards the increase was fantastic. Consequently, despite the largest strikes ever recorded in French social history (150 million working days lost), industrial production in 1968 was on average 4·5 per cent higher than in 1967.

Similarly in the spring of 1971 two million working days were lost between April and June – an enormous total. There were

strikes at Renault, at Usinor, on the railways, as well as the
nationwide one-day stoppages called by the CGT and CFDT
in support of demands for retirement at sixty. The Renault
strike lasted over a month, and reduced the production of cars by
23 per cent, but there was a recovery from July to October. The
recovery was only partial at Renault: the company produced
2 per cent more vehicles in 1971 than it had in 1970 (which was a
markedly smaller increase than in previous years). Between the
Renault strike and the wave of other strikes in the spring of 1971,
overall production was slowed down by something between 1 and
2 per cent; but this was remedied in the second half of the year by
a leap forward of 4 to 5 per cent. These 1971 strikes are the only
ones since 1968 to have produced any visible (though temporary)
disruption in the French economy as a whole.

Other strikes have an effect restricted to their own sector
of the economy, and in such cases losses are always made up over
the next few months. As instances of this we may cite the
Rhodiaceta strike in March 1967, the miners' strike in Faul-
quemont, Auchel and Bruay in February 1971, the strike at the
Potasses d'Alsace at the end of 1972, the Renault strike in 1973
(which caused as great a loss of production to the company
itself as the 1971 strike, but had no noticeable effect on the economy as a whole). The cement-workers' strike at the end of 1973
had certain peculiar features: the production of building materials
was down 10 per cent in November and December as against
October; it recovered in January, when it was 14 per cent up on
October. So far, nothing unusual. But the strike affected building
and public works, not in November, when contractors were still
using up their stocks, but in December – when activity went down
by 10 per cent. And recovery was also delayed – to February,
rather than January – since the cement works could not meet
delivery dates.

On the other hand, numbers of quite large strikes (large in
terms of the number of working days lost) have no apparent
economic effects at all: electricians' strikes never reduce the
amount of electricity produced, and the French national inter-
industry strikes (March 1969, December 1971, June and October
1972, December 1973) never halted the growth of industrial

production (except when, as in the spring of 1971, they were combined with strikes in major companies).

Finally, it is hard to estimate the effect of strikes in the transport and service sector. Industrial action by railwaymen (in France, 200,000 days lost in September 1969, over a million in June 1971), dockers (throughout 1971), air traffic controllers (March 1973), bank clerks (700,000 days lost in March–April 1974) or postal workers (2 to 3 million days lost from October to December 1974) causes obvious and immediate inconvenience. But there is no reason to believe that it has any serious effect on the growth of industrial production or gross domestic product (services included). When it is taking place, the industrial production index does not go down significantly. I can think of only two exceptions. The French railway strike in June 1971 was part of a whole wave of strikes, and its specific effects cannot be estimated. The French postal strike at the end of 1974 accompanied a drop in production; however, it did not cause it, but in the view of some observers may have reinforced it.

To sum up, then, a strike only constitutes sabotage in the firm where it takes place. At that level it can produce an irreparable loss of production, or at least a serious slowing-down of growth. At the level of the sector of the economy, or the economy as a whole, strikes at worst lead to no more than a delay in production (a fall followed by a recovery). So, as a general phenomenon, the strike is only a temporary form of sabotage.

Such are my conclusions in relation to France. However, two Canadian researchers, estimating the loss of production in Canada at the level of sectors of the economy, have reached slightly different conclusions about production recovery. According to them, something under 1 per cent of the nation's production is lost due to strikes; it does not appear either that firms show increased production just before strikes or that they make up the lost production afterwards.

In Great Britain the effect of strike action on production became a major issue in the mid-sixties. It was widely believed that putting a stop to strikes would solve the economic problems of British industry. This question was at the centre of the investigations carried out by the Donovan Commission. There were two conflicting viewpoints: one held that the number of wildcat strikes, and the fact that these were unpredictable and could involve large numbers of workers in key jobs, was very damaging. The other emphasized the limited effect of strikes and held that absenteeism (whether through sickness or industrial accidents) has a much more damaging effect on production. Furthermore, the supporters of the latter view believed that strikes were often followed by a period of recovery. It is important to distinguish between various types of strikes: short strikes involving large numbers of workers will always have less effect than a long strike involving, say, a few thousand dockers.

An examination of the statistics of production and strikes in recent years confirms the second view and my general conclusion (that strikes have little effect on the overall economy). 1972 was the record year for strikes in Britain (more than 23 million working days lost); at the same time it was also a year in which there was a level of growth in production which has not been equalled since. In 1972 the months of January and February saw most strike action (50 per cent of the total number of days lost that year). Production fell in February by about 10 per cent but there was a net recovery in the months which followed. August and September saw another upsurge in strike activity (25 per cent of the year's total of days lost) but during these months production continued to grow. The same situation prevailed in 1973. The majority of strikes took place in March (more than 1 million days lost) but production increased in comparison with February – in fact, it has never been bettered since. In February–March 1974 the miners' strike lost 6 million working days, 50 per cent of the days lost that year. In spite of this strike and the three-day week, industrial production did not fall but, on the contrary, rose in February and again in March. The oil crisis began to have an effect in the second half of 1974, and production fell. In 1975 and 1976 activity was almost stagnant, maintaining 1970 levels. 1975 and 1976 were relatively strike-free (4·7 million working days lost in 1975 and 3·2 million in 1976), but this was not sufficient to give a boost to industrial activity.

In the last decade, strike activity would appear to have followed the course of industrial production, increasing during years of economic expansion and falling off in periods of recession. Massive strike action, then, in Britain as in France, has little effect on overall economic performance, although it may have some at local level. One can conclude either that industrial production is completely insensitive to massive striked action (summer 1972, March 1973, February–March 1974) or that a temporary fall in activity resulting from a wave of strikes is followed by recovery, as at the beginning of 1972.

Several questions still remain to be considered. Has the situation always been the same? What tactics can strikers use to try to increase the effects of their work-stoppages, to block production more effectively? How does the recovery of production, normally found after a strike, operate?

How can production be stopped effectively?

A first tactic is to keep a check on supplies of raw materials or component parts: by preventing their delivery, blocking the factory gates when they arrive, preventing access to stores and warehouses, seeking the active support of workers in factories further up the production chain whether belonging to the same company or not. This kind of action can lead to curious games of hide-and-seek. Suppose a company where a strike has been going on for several weeks wants to get deliveries of coal in before the winter. The first thing is to obtain the services of a non-union carrier. The strikers are picketing, and stop the lorry from coming in. The employer then tries to get coal delivered by rail. He will fail, because of the solidarity among the various trade unions (Karsh, 1958). There is a form of action, to be found only in England, very close to this tactic of stopping supplies: 'supportive blacking'. This consists in calling a strike in a firm where there is no dispute, in order to prevent its delivering merchandise to a firm where direct action cannot be organized in order to make the management there see reason. The further such a blacking process is taken, the greater will be the drop in production.

A second tactic is an indefinite strike of an entire plant. It is disruptive to output in the same proportion as it is long, unanimous, called without warning, supported by picketing, occupation or confiscation of tools (in a chair-makers' strike in 1883, the strikers removed the scabs' tools to prevent their working). One such form of action which has disappeared in our time – blacklisting one factory and calling a total strike there, while being prepared to sign on temporarily for one of its competitors – dates back to the seventeenth century: in 1638, solely on the ground that their lunchtime glass of wine had been withdrawn, the journeyman joiners of Dijon blacklisted the town, and for two years no joiners would work there at all (Benoist, 1970). The silk-weavers of Lyon used it after the failure of their two insurrections in 1831 and 1834:

> The weavers laid a ban on the recalcitrant manufacturers. So remarkable was the unity among the workers that no boycotted manufacturer could get any orders filled. Weavers' delegates made regular visits to the workshops to ensure that the decisions of their Friendly Society were carried out. If workers persisted in disregarding them, the delegates would cut their thread [Perdu, 1974].

This sort of action was common in the late nineteenth and early twentieth century, which explains the extraordinary length of the strikes of the period. The ban could be permanent: the hatters in one factory in the Drôme refused to return to work in 1884 after a strike had failed, and the employer was forced to recruit a new workforce (Pierre, 1973). We find this form of action in the United States at that time, too, prompted by the new unskilled workers' unions.

The tactic of the partial strike can sometimes be just as disruptive of production. This may consist in a 'stop and go', a series of repeated stoppages, at regular or irregular intervals, by one or all sections of the staff. (In Italian this is a *sciopero a singhiozzo*, hiccuping strike.) Then there is the spreading strike (*sciopero a sacchiera*, or chess-board strike, in Italian), with the action shifting from one department to another or one trade to another. If regular intermittent strikes are combined with spreading strikes, paralysis will ensue fairly rapidly: ultimately there is no more than a semblance of work between stoppages and no serious production can take place. 'Thrombosis-strikes' in factories where processes are closely interconnected are the result of the same tactic – blocking a key sector in order to disrupt the whole. That key sector could be a particular workshop or an essential service (the electrical system, the computer, movement of goods inside the factory itself). The strikes at Renault, at Usinor, at the Houillères de Lorraine and the 1973 bank strike all popularized this kind of blocking action, with work being gradually brought to a halt on either side of the blocked sector. Such partial strikes can be reinforced by putting machines out of commission without actually destroying them. In 1908, to counter a railwaymen's strike, the Médoc Railway Company tried to set up a substitute service, only to find that the water valves of the locomotives had been taken out and hidden. At Lip in 1973 a similar tactic was used in the context of a total work stoppage: vital components of machines were removed and taken away to prevent any unofficial restoration of production; they were replaced intact when the dispute was over. The same thing was done in Britain by the AUEW in dispute with the *Daily Express* in 1977.

The final tactic for effectively paralysing production is to seize the stocks of the finished product to prevent goods already made from reaching the customer. Customers, too, may show their solidarity by refusing to accept goods from factories where there is a strike. In the Roberts Arundel strike in 1967–8 a million workers threatened to strike in sympathy with the 145 workers in one factory. So totally were their products boycotted that the firm had to close down that factory at the end of the strike (Arnison, 1970).

Have work-stopping tactics developed since the beginnings of the workers' movement? Has their effect on production always been the same? Blacking one factory, combined with the strikers' going to work for other factories, is an effective way of making an employer see reason. A long indefinite strike was the most usual tactic up until the Second World War; during that period strikes lasted on average over ten days, and prolonged disputes resulted in a loss of production – in sabotage, in other words. Since 1945 strikes have become shorter: the average, varying from year to year, has gone down, to a few days or even a day. Since then, lowered output has resulted from partial and combined strikes, which can be extremely disruptive when organized with that aim in view; they also have a better cost/effect ratio from the workers' point of view. In fact, workers today have a whole arsenal of methods enabling them effectively to paralyse the production of their factories whenever they wish. But this potential for organized chaos is far from being realized in all strikes: fewer than 20 per cent last more than a week (that is including both indefinite strikes and recurrent partial strikes). And even in that 20 per cent the strikers do not always risk carrying their decision to stop work to its logical conclusion. In other words, an industrial strike can fulfil the conditions for sabotaging production; the weapons for doing so exist; in recent times – and all over Western Europe – strikers have been making more use of them; but it is still only a minority who do so.

When such sabotage does take place, is it just temporary?

The recovery of production after the return to work

Is the loss of production that is caused by a proportion of strikes permanent? As we have seen, there is often an extra spurt of activity in the months following a return to work. Where and how does this catching-up process take place? There are several different levels to be considered: the plant or the yard where the strike has occurred, other sites belonging to the same firm and other firms in that sector of industry (cf. Knowles, 1954; Chamberlain *et al.*, 1954; Hyman, 1972; Fisher, 1973; Saglio and Tabuteau, 1971).

The employer who wants to make up the loss of production caused by a strike in one of his plants must first take account of the technical limitations both of the product and of his production capacity. He considers first the state of his stock, since the problem of catching up only arises if the loss of production is greater than the volume of stock, or has reduced it to too low a level. He then considers the production capacity of the striking unit: was it being fully used or not? In France it would normally not be, since our industry for the most part works well within the capacity of the available machinery (increased production can be achieved by employing more workers). There is, finally, a third limitation to be reckoned with, this time on the marketing side:

the employer will only try to make up lost production if the orders he had in hand before the strike began have not since been cancelled.

In practice, the employer can sometimes guard against some of the consequences of a work stoppage if he sees it coming: in that case the lost production can be made up for ahead of time. It can sometimes even be made up during the strike, if a minimum of work is ensured by non-strikers, managerial staff and perhaps temporary labour employed for the purpose. The firm can also maximize production in other plants where there is no strike, providing they make the same products. But in most cases the making up of lost production is in fact a recovery – that is to say, it takes place after the return to work.

Increased output after a strike can be achieved by various means: the commonest is simply getting more hours worked (recovering the hours lost by the strike with overtime working or taking on more men – more hours are also worked because of the temporary reduction in absenteeism noticeable after so many strikes). The second means is the intensification of work: the pace of operations is speeded up, management do their best to reduce timewasting and the workers, for their part, work faster and stop less often, as always after a time of idleness. If the strike has resulted in establishing a happier atmosphere in the factory – by improving negotiating methods, for instance – then this too may lead to increased productivity. This sort of recovery of production, coupled with improvement in the quality of work, takes place without any reorganization. But an employer may also decide, following a strike, to invest in improvements which will ultimately increase productivity. 'Strikes stimulate technological progress, by so annoying and disgusting industrialists that they are led to replace human beings, who can strike, with machines, which cannot' (Goetz-Girey, 1965).

This pattern, whereby lost production is made up so that a strike is only temporary sabotage, is the classic one. But workers are now beginning to pay more attention to that return-to-work period: it is no longer unusual to find them deciding to refuse to work overtime to make up for the hours lost in the strike, to go slow or to increase their absenteeism. However, this new trend has not yet become strong enough to prevent the recovery so often to be found in production figures.

We have still to examine one final factor that reduces the importance of strikes in sabotaging production: a strike may cause a particular product to disappear from the market for a time. If the firm concerned has a monopoly or the product is unique, then there is effectively a temporary fall in production. That is the exception; more often the demand will shift to something else – customers will turn to competing products as a substitute, and the output of other firms in that sector of industry then rises. The postal strike at the end of 1974 resulted in great strides being made by other means of communication (telephones and telex). Such shifts and substitutions in demand explain why some strikes – which, though major, are restricted to a single company – have no perceptible effect on the growth of industrial production in the sector of the economy involved.

So, to return to the question we asked first: are strikes sabotage, resulting in a noticeable loss of production? Most writers on the subject would say no, basing their reply on the fact that production figures rarely fall perceptibly during strikes, and then when they do, recovery usually occurs afterwards. I would not deny all this, but I do think there are certain distinctions to be drawn: a minority of strikes *do* constitute effective sabotage at the level of the plant or yard where they occur – though almost never beyond it; they generally involve the use of methods which tend to paralyse production, and strikers are beginning to look at the problem of preventing recovery afterwards. In other words, in recent years, strikes have developed as a means of sabotaging production; their effect on production may ultimately be far greater than it is now, and is already greater than it was at the turn of the century.

Slowing down production

We have discussed destructive sabotage, and sabotage to stop production and prevent its being made up subsequently. A final form of sabotage is that of slowing down production. Without actually bringing production to a halt, workers can reduce it to a greater or lesser extent. They can also reduce the quality of the goods produced while not making them unsaleable. They may achieve this effect by going slow, by outright reduction of working hours, working to rule, working without enthusiasm, absenteeism, high labour turnover or refusal to enter the job-market at all.

Going slow

If it results in a permanent lowering of production, this is sabotage. It used to be called 'ca'canny' in Britain and is known by many names in other countries; it is as old as industrialization itself. Émil Pouget has made a study of its origins, and believes it began in Scotland in 1889. The Glasgow dockers went on strike, and were replaced by farmworkers who did the job far less well. On returning to work, having failed to get the wage-increase they had asked for, the dockers copied the farmworkers and handled only half the normal amount of goods. So going slow or 'gently' or 'Ca'canny' began. The theory was produced in 1895: when wages are low, provide inferior or poor-quality goods; poor work for poor pay. Ca'canny was thus both a slowing down of work and a deterioration of quality. The most pointed instance was when the Beaford construction workers in the US in 1908, on having their wages reduced, cut the size of their shovels proportionately: 'Small shovels for small wages.'

But, in fact, the practice is far older. F. W. Taylor, the father of scientific work organization, declared that

underworking, that is, deliberately working slowly so as to avoid doing a full day's work, 'soldiering' as it is called in this country, 'hanging it out' as it is called in England, 'ca cannae' as it is called in Scotland, is almost universal in industrial establishments, and prevails also to a large extent in the building trades. [The workman] deliberately plans to do as little as he safely can . . . in many instances to do not more than one third to one half of a proper day's work [F. W. Taylor, 1909].

Nowadays going slow can take various forms: a fall in production results when work is done either more slowly or for a shorter time. So workers may decide on a certain pace; alternatively they may decide how much they will do before they stop, as when, in the spring of 1975, the workers who printed *Le Parisien libéré* decided to produce no more than 50 per cent of the normal number of copies.

We may sort the various types of go-slow into categories. In the first case, the management is prevented from establishing any production quotas because the workers refuse to cooperate and down tools the moment time-and-motion personnel appear. The management of Massey-Ferguson found an answer to this tactic in 1970: the standards department ordered work to be done at a pace no one could possibly keep up. To prove that it was an insane regulation, the workers had to call in the time-and-motion people they had refused to allow in earlier on, who could then time them at their jobs. So a way had been found to circumvent this ploy. But there is a more generalized opposition to norm-setting: it may take the form of putting pressure on the time-and-motion personnel, slowing down the machinery (when the workers are in control of it) or intentional inefficiency – doing things in a more leisurely way, and taking additional measures supposedly to ensure safety or quality, against the stated regulations laid down by the production department (Rolle, 1962).

A second form of action is the decision for each person to work at his or her own 'natural' pace. It may be approved temporarily or permanently at the end of a strike (as with the CGCT telephone construction company and Devanlay Recoing knitwear in 1971, Confection Coframaille, Société Parisienne de Lingerie Indémaillable and Jaeger automobile fittings in 1972).

A third form of go-slow consists in determining a collective pace that is the same for everyone and considerably below the demands of the management: in this case the workers reduce production to a level that does not seriously cut down wages (beyond a certain level wages increase much more slowly than the extra goods produced). They may decide to take their breaks all at the same time, or take a longer break than is permitted. And they may stop the assembly-line a number of times during the course of the day (as at La Redoute in 1970; but there the management found a solution – the switches were linked to a system that made it possible to detect the point at which the current was turned off). There are hidden breaks that cause the loss of more production time than organized breaks – time spent by workers doing things other than their job (blowing their noses, for instance) or things accessory to them (adjusting machines, sharpening tools). Some German researchers have estimated that breaks of this kind may take up to 10 to 20 per cent of the whole time spent at work (Sartin, 1970).

A fourth form of go-slow relates to the way the work of individuals is organized: so that the firm can keep an eye on their output, workers may be required to hand in work-slips at the end of each day with the amount of work they have done written on them. The 'slip strike' (as at Confection Manufacture de Blainville in 1972) consists in not filling them in, tearing them up, or refusing to hand them in. Since the firm then has no means of checking up, the pace of work can be slowed down, as described above. Direct action of this kind is fairly widespread, but is not necessarily connected with any effort to change the nature of the work done to something less fragmented and repetitive.

Strictly speaking, a go-slow means reducing production to its technical minimum. It can involve damage both to machinery and to goods. This action is used in factories where there is continuous production: thus the workers at Lacq SNPA in 1975 reduced gas production by several million cubic metres a day. It is also an established form of action in the French Electricity Council. Current can be cut off from houses and factories without a total shut-down of power stations. Whenever there is a strike, there is discussion between the local management and the trade union leadership. They work out a compromise on the minimum current to be supplied; and, since it *is* a compromise, the minimum is always higher than what technical constraints would impose (Barrier, 1975).

A final form of go-slow is the stopping of machines by deliberate error on the part of the operators, without damaging either equipment or goods. This practice is traditional in the textile industries. The machines (spinning and twisting machines, warping-frames, weaving looms) all have automatic stopping mechanisms which function when a thread breaks. If a worker purposely breaks a thread, the loom or spindle stops just as it does in the case of an accidental break.

Unilateral direct action to reduce working time is also a kind of go-slow, since no production takes place during the hours not being worked. Thus, workers sometimes collectively decide on a different timetable from the one in force in the factory: they may cut down the week's working time by leaving their places several hours early at the end of the week (as in Electricité de France at Rennes in 1969, or the Banque de France at Chamalières in 1975, when the week was cut from 38 hours 20 minutes to 35 hours – i.e. cut by forty minutes a day); they may refuse to work over-time (as did the French dockers in 1971 and the British miners in 1973 and 1974), to work on Sundays (Papeterie Zig-Zag in 1972) or on Saturdays (Verrerie Domec in 1971); or they may take more than the specified number of breaks (PJT textiles in 1971). However, it is most unlikely that the drop in production was proportionate to the drop in working hours: not all working time is equally productive, and overtime working is often less efficient.

Finally, going slow can be virtually institutionalized, as has happened in Great Britain. An unwritten code of 'custom and practice' exists in every industry, consisting of tacit agreements as to procedures and pace of work, the degree of supervision by the hierarchy, and methods of payment. Their existence undoubtedly has the effect of reducing productivity: British employers consistently try to pare them down, as in the policy of productivity bargaining in the middle 1960s.

Has there been an increase in the frequency of these various forms of go-slow since the last century? A comparison of events in the French postal service, to take one instance, makes one wonder. There was a go-slow by Paris postmen as long ago as 1793 (Frischmann, 1967); in 1889 there was a go-slow on the Paris telegraph switchboard, when all the operators were present and *seemed* to be working normally, but were in fact not really transmitting the texts of the telegrams at all. In 1927 a go-slow was organized by the postal federation of the CGTU (the

Communist-controlled confederation of that period): 'As a first step in response to low pay and pay reductions: carry out your day's work methodically, sensibly, slowly but surely. Only do what you absolutely have to do. Everyone should observe all the regulations. They are your safeguard. Carry them out to the letter ...' In 1971 there was a strike of telecommunications technicians: communications were hampered by blocking the telephone switchboards of selected businesses and government offices with fake calls. At the end of 1974 there was a postal strike; after the return to work, as a protest against non-payment for the days of the strike, postal workers handled only half the normal amount of mail per hour, thus delaying distribution still further. Thus over 200 years we find forms of action that are substantially the same.

However, it seems that there has been a certain development in methods over the past few years. Refusal to hand in time-slips has recently become a significant tactic. It is new for go-slow techniques to be tailored to suit the industry concerned, thus joining those forms of industrial action whose aim is to establish a cost-efficiency ratio favourable to the workers concerned. In the absence of any statistics, since nowhere have figures for go-slow actions been compiled, one can only refer to specific studies: in our study of strikes (Dubois and Durand, 1975), we found there had been go-slows in a third of the 123 firms in our sample. In a more restricted study I made of some ten new factories (Dubois, 1974a), I found instances of going slow in three quarters of them: reductions in the collective pace of work (throughout the day, at certain times, by prolonging break-times, or by stopping or slowing down the assembly-line), an appearance of activity where there is none (this is a form of action used by setters: they seem to be busy, but are in fact continually undoing the settings they have made), reducing the amount of repetitive work required (in one place the workers soldered only four out of every five joints, in another they only assembled every other item, with the components of the alternative ones reaching the end of the line unassembled).

The longest go-slow in all these firms was fifteen days. Is it only a temporary phenomenon? Is it, in fact, sabotage, really involving loss of production? Considered in isolation, it is probably not very significant, but in combination with the other forms of action we shall next consider, it is by no means negligible.

Working to rule

Like the go-slow, the work-to-rule was recognized at the turn of the century. Pouget boasted of the 'obstructionism' of the Italian railwaymen in their great strike in 1905. Without stopping work, they seriously disrupted the movement of passengers and freight; in this sense, it was sabotage. Their tactic was to carry out to the letter all the regulations laid down for their work – regulations normally ignored so that the service could function properly. They closed and opened ticket-offices only at the specified times; they made passengers produce the exact fare for their tickets; they carried out all the prescribed checks before allowing the trains to start (marking certain carriages as out of use after the train had been made up, insisting on the three regulation lamps on all tenders, refusing to depart unless all the carriages were immaculately clean and every single door and window properly shut, etc.) so that departures might be delayed for several hours.

Working to rule has remained a tradition in the railways. It is still the form of action most used by railwaymen in Britain. But it can be effective in any of the services, and in all administrative departments in which regulations of great precision are laid down but found in practice to be impossible to observe. In recent times in France there have been work-to-rules by customs-men, the clerks who pay out family allowances, and air traffic controllers. These last, by their action in 1971, indubitably had an effect on the amount of air traffic; but the effect was reckoned to be insufficient, and, despite the fact that strikes were excluded by their contracts, the controllers went on to stop work altogether in the spring of 1973.

Just how did they work to rule to disrupt services in 1971? It was simply a matter of going against all usual practice by carrying out to the letter all the international civil aviation regulations. This at once produced delays in take-offs and landings, sometimes of more than an hour. These regulations included the spacing out of landings, the slow and careful repetition of all the identification code letters of every plane (which soon jammed all the available radio frequencies), making contact with each plane every time it lost three hundred metres' altitude, refusing to clear departures until the flight-plan had reached the control tower, systematically slowing things down the moment any untoward incident occurred – insisting on the removal of a scrap of tyre from the runway before allowing further take-offs, for instance (Bourdet, 1974).

Working without enthusiasm

'Working without enthusiasm' is a way of slowing production that involves no clear infringement of the norms laid down by the firm and is therefore not subject to penalties. It is on the borderline of the permissible: the worker does as much as he has to do to avoid reprimand, but not a fraction more. Even the simplest repetitive job demands a certain minimum of initiative and in this case it is failing to show any non-obligatory initiative that can be considered for our purposes as sabotage, since it leads to a fall in production – above all in quality. The worker carries out every operation minimally; the moment there is a hitch of any kind he abandons all responsibility and hands over to the next man above him in the hierarchy; he works mechanically, not checking the finished object, not troubling to regulate his machine. In short, he gets away with as much as he can, but never actually does anything positively illegal. This was how the Fiat workers who were dissatisfied with their job-descriptions behaved: they did what they were paid for, and were totally apathetic beyond that (Platania, 1974). We were able to make a study of one factory where they made rubber boots, and an examination of the fifty or so different stages which went into the making of the finished product showed that carelessness can occur anywhere, and can have a disastrous effect on quality: from leaving them too long or too short a time in the moulder to an error in heating the rubber so that it comes to pieces on the assembly line; from assembling them slightly crooked to cutting the reinforcements slightly too small; from mixing up the sizes to not checking regularly enough. Even the worker whose job is to glue reinforced soles on with a brush can do it badly: the sole, which should be close-fitting, will flap at the edges if it is not stuck on properly.

Absenteeism

Worker absenteeism causes obvious disruption in production. Every morning, the way each shop management organizes the day's work will depend on which workers are away. There is always coming and going – those who were away return, those who were present the previous day are away. A firm will protect itself against the ill-effects of absenteeism by systematically employing a larger workforce than is theoretically necessary.

The problem is considerable: a Ministry of Labour inquiry in France, which examined 24,000 firms, disclosed that 5·8 per cent of all employees were absent between 21 and 24 October 1974 – due to work accidents, illness or other reasons (and this did not include people absent on holiday or on training courses). The INSEE inquiry, which used a different frame of reference, but was equally representative, showed that 35 per cent of all employees were absent for at least an hour during October 1972. In Great Britain, absence for sickness costs over 300 million working days a year. The General Household Survey conducted in 1972 showed that, on an average, 6·7 per cent of all workers are absent at any one time.

Absenteeism in itself cannot be held to be direct sabotage, taking sabotage to mean something done by workers for the purpose of reducing production. Its causes have been classified as follows: sickness, maternity, accidents at work, and other causes (with or without authorization). Some absences for sickness can be looked on as deliberate refusals to work, and therefore as sabotage – employers complain that doctors often provide certificates on request, but they have no means of knowing *how* often – as can some accidents (known in France as *accidents volontaires*), and all unauthorized absences. Sabotage-absenteeism, i.e. refusal to work resulting in a drop of production, can probably be estimated at about 1 to 2 per cent of the hours which should normally be worked. It is hardly a negligible figure; in fact it is noticeably higher than the proportion of time lost by strikes.

One anarchist worker has recalled the kind of deliberate accidents that commonly occurred at work among revolutionaries at the turn of the century. (The French term then was *faire le macadam*, and a similar phrase is used in workers' argot today: *piquer un macadam*, for a simulated accident). Some people use them quite regularly as a way out of difficulties. Every trade has its own catalogue of deliberate accidents, inherent in the nature of the work, and its occupational hazards (sprains, grazes, cuts, etc.). The worker who was hurt would receive insurance money as long as he had a witness and could get a letter from some compliant doctor in return for a share of the money. How long he went on drawing the money depended on his skill in faking or maintaining his wound.

There was a well-tried anti-cure system for keeping injuries going or infecting them, making wounds granulate and suppurate, causing the infected places to swell and become inflamed, in other words to spin out the half-pay. This lore, passed on by word of mouth among friends, was part of the self-defence equipment of many of the working-class [Michaud, 1967].

It is clear from a number of studies that absenteeism has been on the increase in recent years: in France the Ministry of Labour noted a rate of 4·9 per cent in 1951 and 5·8 per cent in 1974. The annual statistics of the National Insurance Fund also show a rise (of about 3·9 per cent) since 1969. The inquiry conducted by the Engineering Employers' Association, UIMM, showed an increase of about 1·5 per cent as between 1968 and 1973. The same pattern emerges in Great Britain: indeed the fact that sanctions systems have developed in so many firms is indication enough of an attempt to stem the increase in the absenteeism rate. On the other hand, the number of working days lost for reasons of certified illness was almost 10 per cent higher in the years 1970–74 than the years 1960–64 (see Chapter 5 below; also Behrend and Pocock, 1976; Nicholson, 1976). The same phenomenon is observable in a lot of industrialized countries – and this in spite of a general improvement in health among the population at large.

However, the fact that absenteeism is on the increase today should not lead us to forget what an old-established practice it is: absenteeism after holidays and at harvest-time was significant in the last century. The employer I quoted earlier (Bergerie), writing in 1830, lamented the absenteeism common in factories; he gave this advice to his colleagues: 'Withholding wages is not enough to deal with repeated absences; the harm they do to a manufacturer by disrupting workshops, and robbing him of a regular return on his investment, makes them utterly intolerable. You must ruthlessly dismiss all your Monday absentees: they cost you at least fifty-two days a year.' Our anarchist worker confirms that at the turn of the century there were people for whom taking Mondays off was a regular habit: 'You ate better and drank better wherever people were regular and enthusiastic devotees of *Saint-Lundi*' (Michaud, 1967).

Labour turnover

Is this a form of sabotage? When it is high, it increases costs and has a negative effect on the volume and quality of production: a new worker works slower, and, until he has developed good 'working habits', less well. But this is not deliberate, so it cannot be called sabotage. The real saboteur could be said to be the man who leaves, and so disrupts production to some extent for a time. But he is probably acting no more deliberately than the novice. Labour turnover as deliberate sabotage by workers is certainly not significant.

Is the turnover rate higher today than it was a century ago? Among the Lyon silk-weavers in 1830, for instance, turnover was the norm – in fact there was no option. A pamphleteer of the period wrote, pityingly: 'You will say, they are free! That is their misfortune. When they are needed, they are hired as cheaply as possible. Once they have finished making the cloth they were wanted for, they are dismissed as easily as they were taken on, with absolute callousness' (quoted in Moissonnier, 1975). The weavers changed workshops every two weeks or so. F. W. Taylor gives a turnover rate of 40 per cent for some American firms at the turn of the century, but they were firms where scientific methods of work organization were not in use; in those where Taylorian principles were applied, he tells us, the rate was almost nil. This seems open to doubt: early this century, the success of the Ford Model T enabled Henry Ford to revise his company's production methods. The assembly-line was introduced for the first time. It caused dissatisfaction among a great many workers, and they left their jobs; in 1913 the turnover rate was 380 per cent. When the permanent workforce in the Detroit factory had to be increased by 100 at the end of 1913, almost 1,000 had to be signed on because of the rate at which they left. Yet, logically, the turnover rates of that time should have been lower than those of today – the job market then was strictly limited to the town or the particular trade. However, a certain number of workers would choose to become self-employed: Michaud says that this was still quite a common occurrence in the early years of this century. He could no longer remember how many different jobs he himself had held, since he always left when something went wrong, so long as he had enough money put by to live on for a while.

Have rates gone up significantly in recent years? It is hard to say, in the absence of any overall statistics. Rates vary enormously from one firm to another, a tiny percentage in some, over 100 per cent in others.

Refusal to work

The various forms this can take are all alike in that all represent a withdrawal from the industrial scene: wage-earners indirectly sabotaging production by refusing to take factory jobs, and thus – especially in times of full employment – disrupting the whole organization of labour. This has increased in recent years. It is similar to the situation in the last century when some men preferred vagabondage to factory work.

First there is the preference for non-industrial work. There are seldom more people wanting jobs in industry than there are jobs offered, and certainly not the large disproportion found in business and services (where there was an average of six or seven applicants for every job in France in 1974, compared with only two in industry).

Second, there is avoidance of employment. Some people, though of course it is hard to estimate how many, are quite content to enrol at the employment exchange and receive unemployment pay which in some cases enables them not just to subsist, but to live quite comfortably. The overall increase in jobs available in France since 1969 may perhaps be partly attributable to this tendency to opt for paid non-work. There are two other significant points in this connection. First, there has been an enormous increase in unemployment among young people even before they have held any job at all. This cannot simply be explained in terms of the economic situation and the fact that their education has not equipped them for the job market. Young people's allergy to work can take different forms (Rousselet, 1974): taking temporary work of no interest or importance, avoidance of employment, failing to look for a job on leaving school, dropping out of apprenticeships or training courses for no particular reason. The second thing that seems to suggest that many prefer not to work is that the average length of time for which people draw unemployment pay is increasing. This is not solely due to the general job shortage. It would appear that, despite the fact that labour exchanges are successfully placing more applicants than ever, some people are reluctant to accept the jobs offered them. Alongside the many who feel ashamed to be out of work, there are others who prefer it and see it as a good thing.

Finally there is the fact that the proportion of people at work in certain age-groups has gone down (in particular, people are starting work later and retiring earlier); this seems to suggest a move away from productive work, and not only a consequence of later school-leaving and better retirement conditions. This reduction is, however, largely compensated for by a higher proportion of women working in all age groups.

Summary

Going slow, workers' decisions to cut down on hours, working without enthusiasm, absenteeism, labour turnover and simply not working, all these things consistently serve to reduce production. When they include an element of deliberate choice on the part of the workers, they may be classed as sabotage; so it is only in some cases that absenteeism, leaving jobs, or refusing to work are actually sabotage. But there are several indications that for quite a long time now the number of such instances has been on the increase.

Practices like these, less concentrated in time but in some cases fairly continuous, can do more damage than strikes – which, as we have seen, do not always lead to even a temporary drop in production. Strikers are sometimes hesitant to go all out to stop manufacture or deliveries, nor do they always have the means to prevent the process of recovery that always follows a long strike. Some strikes – not all – are sabotage, but usually with only a short-term effect.

Destroying machinery and goods is obviously sabotage, in that it reduces both the quality and the quantity of production. A sabotaged product is lost for good; a sabotaged machine is useless and unproductive until it is repaired. The damage done by such destruction is limited by its extreme rarity, but nonetheless instances have occurred throughout the history of the workers' movement.

Is the harm done to production by these various forms of sabotage of major significance overall? One would think so, to judge from the impassioned things people say about it. But if one looks at the economic evidence, the answer is not so clear: in France, for instance, the volume of production lost through destruction (including theft) is hard to estimate precisely, but is certainly less than 1 per cent a year; strikes and restrictive practices cause a loss of less than 0.5 per cent, absenteeism 1 per cent and labour turnover perhaps about the same. Working without enthusiasm and lack of initiative are extremely harmful forms of sabotage, but it is often very hard to prove anything against anyone. The effect on production will, of course, vary with the situation: a deliberate reduction of activity when the order-book is empty does not have the same effect as when it is important to meet delivery dates. The probability is that the loss of production is somewhere between 1 and 3 per cent a year.

Let me conclude by stressing a somewhat paradoxical correlation: even though, overall, forms of sabotage have never been as numerous as they are today, increases in productivity have never been so great. In France the ratio between the value added by manufacture and the activity of the workforce (calculated as the product of the number of persons employed and their hours of work) has been rising from an annual average of 4·6 per cent in 1949 to as high as 5·7 per cent annually between 1967 and 1972 (Brunhes, 1974). In fact the indicator of work productivity cannot directly measure the incidence of sabotage, since it takes account only of goods actually produced and hours actually worked. By definition, production lost through sabotage does not figure in statistics of effective production, and hours not worked (due to strikes, absenteeism or unemployment) are ignored in statistics of working hours. We could only measure the incidence of sabotage if we had an index that included non-production and non-work, and no such index exists.

Nevertheless, one can build a fairly solid hypothesis on such data as there are. Just as cutting down the number of hours worked is often reckoned as a factor in increased productivity because it also reduces fatigue, so too it may well be that some forms of sabotage also have a beneficial effect on productivity (reduction of fatigue due to a slowing-down of production, to strikes and to absenteeism; fresh investment and new methods of organizing work following industrial activity by workers). So we may conclude this chapter on a note of paradox: sabotage reduces production in the short term, but ultimately contributes to increasing it.

In this chapter, we have distinguished three forms of sabotage, according to the type of damage they cause: destroying machinery or goods; stopping production; slowing down work. In the following chapters we shall be using other classifications for different purposes: for instance, active sabotage involves some action on the part of the worker, a physical action or movement, whereas passive sabotage implies the opposite – inaction (e.g., seeing that a machine is out of order and failing to inform the maintenance department). There is offensive sabotage, which is part of workers' strategy in their struggle against management; there is spontaneous sabotage, which its authors have not thought out in advance; and there is organized sabotage – that is to say, sabotage carried out by a group.

2 The Aims of Sabotage

What is the reason for sabotage? Any industrial action may have two elements to it: it may be aimed at a limited or total transformation of the present situation (in which case it has an instrumental character); alternatively, it may expose the evils of the situation without changing it, or illustrate the possibility of a different sort of society (in which case it has a demonstrative character). Thus, instrumental sabotage is sabotage directed to the achievement of certain limited demands and/or a change of political power in society. Demonstrative sabotage is not out to achieve any practical result for its perpetrators, but expresses a wish to castigate the management, a protest against injustice, a rejection of accepted values; it may also paint a picture of what life could be like for workers in a socialist society.

Instrumental sabotage with limited objectives can be part of a strategy for pursuing demands. It may be directed to one or more, latent (implicit) or explicit, objectives, to one issue or several (in which case one may have priority or all may be of equal importance), to a long-planned aim or one that has been formulated on the spur of the moment. If it is defensive, it may be in anticipation of possible action by management to worsen workers' conditions (a go-slow may be operated to forestall a review of the payments system); or it may be the response to a decision already made by management that goes against workers' interests (the suppression of some previously won right, or a new repressive measure), in which case the aim is to get the decision reversed. If it is offensive, then it results from a free decision by the workers: it may or may not be part of a strategy of escalation (the use of increasingly intensive sabotage); it may be a bargaining counter, a form of blackmail or a strident way of attracting public attention. In defensive sabotage, action by workers follows action by management; in offensive sabotage, the workers' initiative comes first.

Separate mention must be made of direct action as instrumental sabotage. Sabotage may stimulate management to make concessions, but some forms of sabotage actually effect the desired change. In the former case management makes the decision to change, and there may or may not be previous negotiation with the saboteurs. But in the latter there is no negotiation: the change in the workers' status is imposed by force and takes place immediately – i.e., by direct action. For instance, a go-slow – which is sabotage in so far as it lowers production – may be intended to reduce the burden of work. The aim in view is achieved at once, simply by putting the go-slow into effect. The result may be ratified by negotiation, afterwards, but has already been attained.

What are in practice the kinds of demands which sabotage is used to support? The worker may try to add to his earnings (by theft) or to receive payment without having to work for it (if a factory burns down, then he is technically out of work, and receives unemployment pay; voluntary unemployment eventually leads to receiving unemployment pay; absenteeism seldom results in any loss of earnings nowadays). The aim may be to get the working day organized differently from the way the firm now organizes it (more free time, more freedom to plan one's own time, shorter working hours), or it may be a question of ensuring a guaranteed number of hours' work, of lightening the work-burden, of reducing the restrictions imposed by management, of varying the monotony of certain tasks. All these aims may coexist, and the demand may then take the form of demanding a collective agreement.

Instrumental sabotage for political objectives (i.e., aiming to change the government) is seldom presented as such. We have seen only two instances of it in the history of France: the revolutionary general strike of CGT members at the beginning of this century had as its explicit aim 'the total emancipation of the proletariat'; and the sabotage in the Second World War was intended explicitly to hasten the defeat of the German occupiers and the overthrow of the Vichy régime. On the other hand, the context in which it occurs can cause sabotage to take on a political dimension and lead to an overthrow of the government without its having begun with that aim in view. That is likely to happen when there is an escalation strategy (with one sabotage leading to another) or when the sabotage, instead of remaining isolated, spreads to a wider area.

Demonstrative sabotage is not demanding any improvement in working conditions – but this does not mean that it is simply gratuitous. It is expressing a real discord, a class enmity. It may be sheer vengeance, the only thing left to do when all else has failed, a cry of despair, a last gasp: 'The boss has attacked us, and we are having our revenge on his goods.' It can also be a way of indicating that the interests of owners and workers are at variance: 'Why produce good quality, work enthusiastically, economize on materials, do all that is laid upon us, why bother, in short, for a boss who is simply exploiting us?' Sabotage can also be aimed directly at the employer's profits as such, making him lose money for the sake of it.

Demonstrative sabotage can also lead to a fresh look at the established values of industrial society. By bringing production to a standstill, it can be an implicit criticism of the whole of capitalist production and the way it grows; it may, similarly, be a criticism of the over-valuation of work as such. Vandalising goods can be a criticism of the manufacture of consumer-goods. It can also demonstrate opposition to the technical and social division of labour.

Finally, merely by taking place, demonstrative sabotage can indicate the possibility of a different society, in which working for wages would not exist. It can show the indispensable role of workers in production (by working to rule), suggest a different form of work organization, a different system of payment, a different philosophy of production.

I shall try to analyse the aims of four types of sabotage: destructive sabotage, strikes (those, that is, that lead to at least a temporary drop in production), go-slows and absenteeism. These four have been studied enough for a comparative analysis of their aims to be possible. In addition, I shall analyse the objectives of the frequent acts of sabotage in one particular dispute: Lip in 1973.

For each one of these categories we shall see how far the aims in view are achieved, whether they are instrumental or demonstrative. In addition there is a further possible consequence – the extension of the sabotage itself. As Hannah Arendt says in her essay on violence (1972):

> The danger of violence, even if it moves consciously within a non-extremist framework of short-term goals, will always be that the means overwhelm the end. If goals are not achieved rapidly, the result will be not merely defeat but the introduction of the practice of violence into the whole body politic ... The practice of violence, like all action, changes the world, but the most probable change is to a more violent world.

The aims of destructive sabotage

Machine-breaking in France had one explicit and overriding aim (Manceau, 1969; Fohlen, 1972): to reject mechanization, which gave rise to poverty by the twofold process of downgrading workers, and thus reducing their wages, and causing unemployment. It was defensive sabotage, for it happened after machinery was installed (no one stopped it from being installed – they waited for a time to see what the effect would be); it was a form of direct action, because logically, once the machines were destroyed, there should have been a return to the earlier system of work. In Vienne in 1819 the workers rose against two manufacturers who decided to introduce a mechanical cutter into their mill; they pointed out that, with only four men working it, it could shear, glaze and brush 1,000 ells of cloth in twelve hours, thus putting a large number of people out of work. The machine had become the enemy. At Rethel in 1840 the wool-spinning mills were fully mechanized by the time machine-breaking took place. Rebellion only began when there was unemployment, especially among working-class people who did not belong to the area and who, therefore, could not support themselves on what they could earn from their plots of ground as could the local workers.

Many of the instances of machine-breaking reported by overseers were not accidental. The proletariat of Rethel blamed their appalling poverty, and all the evils of life, not just on the manufacturers but on the jennies that took away jobs and lowered wages: they called them *casse-bras* [a blow of fate]. There was a song to the effect that the great looms must be removed and turned to dust [Manceau, 1969].

In France machine-breaking seems to have been restricted to immediate aims of this kind, with no political element.

In England the situation was very different. We can distinguish two phases in the destruction of machinery and goods, related to two different kinds of aim (Hobsbawm, 1964). In the eighteenth century machine-breaking was regularly employed as a means of negotiation, to get higher wages or to counter attempts by employers to lower wages. It was the most effective form of combat available at a time when trade unions did not exist, when workers largely worked in their own homes (strikes only became important when the craftsman no longer owned his own means of production) and when, both because they were paid too little to have any savings and because strike-breakers were readily used, they could not hold out for long. In the eighteenth century, then, 'collective bargaining by riot' was dictated by the nature of the circumstances.

Luddism, at the beginning of the nineteenth century, encompassed a larger number of objectives (Thompson, 1963). First of all, the demands it included were far wider in scope: it sought both to preserve the *status quo* – before the coming of the machines – and to guarantee further rights for the workers. But it also had an avowed political dimension. Mechanization had made a frontal attack on a whole industrial system, governed by paternalist legislation (including among other things a seven years' apprenticeship to qualify for a trade) and limiting the number of looms one master could use. The advent of machines therefore disrupted all the old methods of work; it reduced the bargaining power of highly skilled workers and involved a considerable lowering of their status by removing work from small workshops to factories (in other words a shift from independence to subordination), and devalued their skill by increasing the division of labour (which both reduced wages and made the work less interesting). Furthermore, mechanization led to less well-finished goods being put on the market and sold unfairly at a much lower price. Machine-breaking was thus a struggle to preserve an old order characterized by work well done, with skilled workers each doing the whole of the job, for adequate wages and with considerable independence. Luddism was not the destruction of machinery for its own sake; the machines of employers who preserved the old order of things were spared.

But Luddism was not just a 'reactionary' practice to preserve an outworn state of things. It was also a struggle to enforce new rights for workers. Mechanization lowered wages, and Luddism was fighting to achieve a minimum legal wage. Mechanization de-skilled work, bringing numbers of women and children into the labour market, and Luddism was fighting to control this process and keep the effects of competition down. Mechanization led to unemployment, and Luddism was fighting to oblige the masters to find work for skilled workers when they were made redundant. Mechanization produced poor-quality goods, and Luddism was fighting to have shoddy goods officially banned from sale. In this sense Luddism was both defensive and offensive. It was a rearguard battle against the irresistible tide of mechanization; it was also the first struggle for the regulation of labour in a new technical system.

Finally, Luddism undoubtedly had a political dimension, which explains its geographical expansion, its simultaneous outbreak in different places, its inter-area organization, its illegality, certain of its demands (e.g., the right of combination, which was then denied) and the support it received from people in the countryside who were not industrial workers at all. It was a revolt of labouring people against the powers that be, which were abrogating the paternalist legislation of the past and fostering an economic policy of *laissez-faire*. In some cases it had a definitely revolutionary character, involving a confrontation between two armed forces – the army of the people against that of the government. However, the political direction of the movement was not always clear to the actors. In fact two contradictory tendencies could be identified: a revolutionary tendency, directed towards overthrowing the system of government, and a constitutionalist tendency directed towards a reform of parliament, that would end by enfranchising the working class. With the end of the Luddite movement, this latter became the dominant tendency, enshrined in Chartism.

What were the results of all the machine-breaking? In terms of halting the tide of mechanization and maintaining the work-relationships of the past, they were nil. At best they amounted to occasionally delaying the process of change. In terms of stimulating a revolutionary movement, they were also nil. But they were to some extent effective in terms of a certain awakening of political consciousness among working people, which took shape in the Chartist movement in England and the revolutions of 1830 and 1848 in France, and also in terms of a demand for new social rights.

Destructive sabotage today, whether of machinery or of goods, consists in most cases of isolated incidents – so it could hardly lead to a change of government. It is never adopted by the trade unions and only occasionally by extreme left-wing groups (cf. Chapter 4 below); thus it is hard to be sure what its explicit objectives are. Such analysis as it has been possible to make suggests that it is generally aimed at a single objective, that it is seldom planned or offensive in character, but tends to be a reaction against something, and usually takes the form of direct action (which directly achieves the intended result). In certain cases it is mainly demonstrative, trying not so much to improve working conditions as to express protest.

For instance, defensive sabotage which is mainly demonstrative sometimes follows an announcement of mass lay-offs. The workers concerned have not managed to organize sufficiently to force the employers to guarantee security of employment. So pieces of cloth are slashed. Shoes are so badly put together that they can only be sold as seconds. The Royal Suite of a ship is smashed up by the workers who have just finished constructing it – and then been sacked. People vent their feelings on whatever is nearest to hand. What matters is to register your disapproval, find a release for frustration, cause trouble to those who are causing trouble to you. Similar forms of sabotage follow strikes that have failed to achieve their aims. You take your revenge on the boss's property in your anger at having lost so much of your earnings for nothing.

Also defensive, but this time in support of definite claims, is the sabotage described by F. W. Taylor. He describes how, in his early days as a foreman, the workers deliberately broke their machines and then complained that it was his fault for forcing them 'to drive the machine so hard that it is overstrained and being ruined'. Taylor knew this was not true. But that is not the point. What the workers intended was, by means of sabotage, to stop Taylor from pushing them. In the concrete, what they were demanding was: (1) the autonomy in their work which his system took away; (2) the preservation of workers' solidarity against a system of competitiveness and increased division of labour; (3) support for a form of work organization that had hitherto worked very well; (4) a tolerable workload, which they feared the new intensive pace of work would make impossible.

The acts of sabotage carried out in the General Motors plant at Lordstown in 1970 were also reactions against a rigid, scientific-management system of work. But, unlike the preceding instances, these were also offensive and sometimes planned. They were directed to a series of objectives, which they put into practice by direct action. Lordstown was a new plant where work organization was the responsibility of a special department of General Motors. The intensification of work there was tremendous – the number of cars assembled each day broke all records. For a time. The workers soon responded with strikes and acts of sabotage. What were their aims? First, they wanted to gain control over their own working hours and have more free time during the day (a lesser burden of work means less fatigue); for this they planned to sabotage one workshop after another, to create the maximum disruption. Their second objective was to make their sabotage fun: with fire-hoses they turned workshops into vast swimming-pools; they had contests to see who was the best saboteur (seeing who could blow up his engine so as to send the bits furthest away). Games like this broke the monotony of fragmented work, and freed the workers from inhibitions and their fear of management (managers barely dared to venture into the workshops involved). Finally, and this is interesting if only for its rarity, this sabotage was also a protest against a specific new process: a new six-cylinder engine was being assembled, hastily designed and flimsy. The Lordstown workers, having vainly suggested ways of improving its quality, decided that they would themselves check each one produced. Their sabotage prevented the engine ever reaching the market: so many engines were rejected for various defects that there was soon nowhere in the workshops to keep them all (Rosow, 1974; Brecher, 1972; Ratgeb, 1974). This particular outburst of sabotage produced results as soon as it was put into operation. Direct action only achieves its objective while it is actually taking place. So we can say that offensive sabotage by destruction generally only produces temporary results. The other forms of destructive sabotage described were not in pursuit of precise demands; they were, so to say, self-sufficient: the workers had the satisfaction of having had their revenge, of having *dared* to maltreat their working equipment.

During the last war sabotage was occasionally carried out in support of a demand, but more usually it was directly political in character: the aim was to hasten the defeat of the German occupiers and the political system that kept them there.

Sabotage at Renault in 1942 had first of all a humanitarian objective: to stop civilians being killed in air raids. Their second aim was to reduce the German war potential (tanks, aeroplane engines, means of transport). 'Everything possible must be done to stop war production whose purpose is to prolong our sufferings and privations' (R. Durand, 1971). On the railways the first aim was to prevent the transport of raw materials and grain to Germany. 'Our honour, our conscience as workers and fathers of families, forbid us to let the produce of our soil and our subsoil go to feed Hitler and his armies, while we and our wives and children are not getting enough to eat' (quoted in Jacquet, 1967). Sabotage was also intended to hasten the defeat of the enemy by destroying his equipment and disrupting his transport system, especially after the allied landings. The sabotaging of telephone lines and cables (Frischmann, 1967) aimed at the same results: to paralyse German troop activities. There is general agreement as to the part played by sabotage in the German defeat in 1944. However, it was important not to do things that would result in a total paralysis of production once the country was liberated. The following advice (dated 16 April 1944) on the military function of the resistance puts the problem in a nutshell:

> Acts of sabotage should seek to put installations out of commission, but only temporarily. They must harm the enemy but must not lead to the complete economic asphyxiation of the large urban centres; try to ensure being in a position to restore things to normal as rapidly as possible after the liberation of the area [quoted in Lévy, 1974].

The aims of sabotage-strikes

I use the term 'sabotage-strikes' to mean strikes causing a marked drop in production for the firms concerned (even though it may be made up later on). We may distinguish three types of sabotage-strikes: long strikes; strikes which may be shorter, but in which the strikers take measures to ensure that the work stoppage is really effective (by the various tactics discussed in the first chapter, including destruction and bringing machines to a standstill); and mass general strikes. What are the objectives aimed at and the results achieved?

Long strikes

One straightforward question: are there certain demands that employers continue to resist for a longer time? In other words, do we find different objectives in long strikes from those at issue in shorter ones? I am concerned here with explicit objectives, which are the only ones that figure in most of the existing analyses.

Very few studies touch on this question. In our study of strikes, we came to the following conclusions: most of the demands relating to employment and working hours were negotiated in short strikes (though it is possible that following the Lip dispute, the length of strikes to save jobs has increased). In disputes of average length, demands relating to wages, working conditions and job-classification were usually at issue. Demands relating to repressive measures against workers or their representatives tended to be involved when strikes were long. However, the correlation between type of demand and length of dispute may be interpreted in two different ways: a strike may be short either because the workers have not determined to fight to the last ditch for the demand they are making, or because the employer gives way immediately. Similarly with long strikes: perhaps the workers are determined to fight on till they win – or perhaps the employer is intransigent.

We find the same problem when it comes to correlating the length of strikes with their results. Are long strikes more effective than short ones? Some say not: 'The longer a strike goes on, the less reason the employer has to give way. Before the strike, it is worth giving way to avoid the harm that would result from a work stoppage. But in proportion as the harm actually done increases and the strike lengthens out, the loss that can be avoided becomes less and less' (Hicks, quoted in Goetz-Girey, 1965).

But the statement that long strikes are ineffective does not seem to apply to France. In the period 1871–90, the strikes that succeeded were the long ones; however, the highest percentage of successes was scored by strikes lasting between seventeen and thirty-two days – 57·4 per cent of the strikes of that length were successes, whereas the percentage for all strikes was only 50·2 per cent (Perrot, 1973). Over the period 1890–1914 there was little difference: if we reckon not only total successes, but settlements when a compromise was reached, the figures are 54·8 per cent as compared with 59 per cent. On the other hand, if we consider only the strikes that ended in total success, then the longer the strike, the less favourable was the result as far as the workers were concerned (Andréani, 1968). From 1919 to 1962, though the overall proportion of failures was gradually increasing, the longer the strike, the greater the chances of success (Goetz-Girey, 1965). There has been no overall study of the contemporary period. In our study of strikes in 1971 we came to rather complex conclusions: 'Short strikes (a week or less) had a larger proportion of negative results than longer strikes, but their proportion of major results was equal. It would seem, therefore, that the prolongation of strikes to some extent shows a shift from poor or negative results to rather better ones.'

Finally, one may conclude that the most effective strikes tend to be those of medium length, and that 'medium length' has shortened considerably throughout the period (in the order of one to ten). Long strikes, the first form of sabotage-strike we are considering here, are not the most effective in achieving the explicit aims proposed. Strikers are well aware that, in such strikes, the nature of the possible gains can change as time goes on. Disputes which start as merely instrumental come to take on a demonstrative character, simply because they receive more public attention. It then becomes important to make it clear to the workers' movement as a whole that you are determined to carry on to the bitter end, even if it cannot mean total victory. Having the courage to struggle becomes more important than the aim for which you are struggling. Such disputes by the same token also take on a clearly political dimension.

Violent strikes

Do disputes in which strikers actively try to find ways of bringing their firms to a standstill have different aims? Do they have different results? M. Perrot points to the incidence of violent actions against property in defensive strikes that are launched as a reaction to management initiatives to dismiss workers or cut down wages. Such strikes also tend to show a larger-than-average proportion of failures. Shorter and Tilly point out that, in the period 1890–1935, violent strikes began with the same objectives as other strikes (violence only occurring after the action had been launched). As for the results, they show more compromises, fewer successes and fewer failures. The decrease of violence in strikes may explain why there is no study of the correlation of violence with results for the period after that.

In our study of strikes in 1971 we put forward some rather complex conclusions about the links between violence and effectiveness:

Workers' illegality and employers' intransigence in negotiating go hand in hand. This may be interpreted in two ways: it may be that the illegality hardens the management position in negotiating, or, on the other hand, management intransigence may provoke the workers to illegality. Both types of link have been found ... In a certain number of strikes illegality is not directly helpful, as it leads to a hardening of the management side in negotiations. But when the strike ends, the concessions made by management tend to be greater when the workers have resorted to illegal activity, particularly if there has been an escalation of violence. Thus radical action is a two-edged weapon: it starts by hardening the employer. If workers' resistance weakens, then the illegality will have been to no avail; if, on the other hand, the workers stand firm and do not hesitate if need be to call for even tougher forms of action, then the results can be considerable. Therefore, and in so far as illegality also provokes repression, the strikers must be able to cope with repression before they can hope to profit from overstepping the bounds of legality.

In the same study, we were also able to show a significant link between violence and struggles against repression by management, and between violence and struggles in which the explicit demands did not fully cover the grievances the workers wanted to air. In other words, there is reason to believe that disputes of this type are not solely instrumental, but also demonstrative, indicating generalized discontent or protest against repression.

The three studies mentioned reached contradictory conclusions: though the effectiveness of strikes which actually stop production seems greater today, one should not interpret this conclusion in any determinist sense. Illegality, to be really successful, must be combined with considerable worker combativity.

Mass general strikes

I use the term 'mass general strike', in this context, to mean a generalized strike that costs the economy a large number of days' production; I do not include national inter-industry strikes for a limited time (which always result in a limited loss). There have been five periods of mass general strikes in France in this century: 1906, 1919–20, 1936, 1947 and 1968. I look also at the 1926 general strike in Britain. I want here to consider not the general causes of these strikes, but only their aims and their results.

1906: From 1871 to 1914 the average number of days lost by strikes was 1,741,000 per year. In 1906 there were 9,439,000 altogether. The general strike planned for 1 May 1906 had an explicit objective: the eight-hour day. Two methods of action were projected: an indefinite strike was to start on 1 May, in order to force the employers to grant the eight-hour day, and from 2 May all those still working would stop after eight hours. This first French general strike had certain remarkable characteristics which have not appeared in any subsequent strikes: it was a strike for just one explicit objective; it was an offensive, planned strike (planned two years earlier, at the C G T congress in Bourges); and it opted for direct action as the means of making its demand (it was not a question of asking the legislature to pass a law to reduce the working day to eight hours, but of workers making their own decision only to work for a specified time). The 1906 strikes were a failure in terms of their explicit objective: the eight-hour day was not won by direct action; however, by a law of 13 July 1906, the authorities decreed that there must be a rest period of twenty-four consecutive hours once a week (a law frequently not observed, however).

The question is whether the 1906 strike had any objectives other than the explicit one – the eight-hour day. It took place in the context of one of the most animated debates of the trade union movement at the time: the debate over the revolutionary general strike. Several congresses had already put forward motions in favour of a liberating general strike that would put an end once and for all to wage-labour and the private ownership system. Would the 1906 strike be *the* strike? The last one? This must have been the question in many people's minds, for there was a flurry of wall-slogans heralding 'X days to freedom'. Yet it would have been naïve in the extreme to think that such a political goal could be set for a particular date. It would seem that the political objective was not so much revolution as to prepare people's minds for revolution by means of the accompanying propaganda. The workers had to be made aware of their own power.

1919-20: The Russian revolution in 1917 and the international situation in 1919–20 brought the problem of revolution back into the forefront; hence there were those (a minority of the C G T) for whom the strikes of 1919 and 1920 were directly revolutionary in purpose; but for everyone else (the C G T majority represented by Jouhaux) they were to make it possible for the workers' movement to advance within capitalist society. The general strike of 1 May 1919, branching out into a series of actions (15·5 million days' strike in 1919 – as compared with an average of 6·8 million from 1919 to 1936) was therefore something of a tussle: the majority wanted it to be directed to getting the eight-hour day just voted by the legislature put into effect at once, whereas the minority wanted it to be the first stage of the revolution. They pressurized the leadership of the C G T (in vain) to call a general strike in July.

In 1920 it was the railwaymen – whose union had, after an earlier strike in February, gone over to the minority side – who gave the impetus for mass action. A general strike on the railways was to start on 30 April 1920, to demand nationalization and the cessation of all disciplinary measures against the February strikers. The railwaymen, wanting to transform this issue-strike into the driving force of a revolutionary movement, sought support from the C G T as a whole. Unlike the previous year, the C G T leadership let themselves in part be persuaded; they called for general strikes of solidarity, to be launched in successive waves, on 3, 10 and 11 May. But, given the poor showing of certain sectors (in spite of which there were a record 23 million days' strike in 1920), the lack of any surprise effect, the fact that nationalization had no appeal to the rank and file, and large-scale repression by the government, the C G T gave the word for a general return to work on 22 May. The railwaymen did not go back until 28 May. Their demands were not met: 18,000 railwaymen were dismissed. The mass general strikes of 1919–20, even more than those of 1906, had different political objectives for each of the tendencies represented in the workers' movement: one wanting merely to put pressure on the authorities, the other to overthrow the bourgeois state power altogether.

1936: In a different set of circumstances (with the advent of the Popular Front government), the 1936 strikes also had a clear political objective as far as the great majority of the workers were concerned: the aim was to force the new government to satisfy as soon as possible the claims tabled earlier by the workers which had figured in their electoral programme. The 1936 strikes (an estimated 30 million working days), unlike earlier mass strikes, achieved results that were far from negligible. The Matignon agreement of 9 June provided for the negotiation of collective agreements, the right to join a union, the appointment of employees' representatives (*délégués du personnel*) in factories, and wage increases of between 7 and 15 per cent. For their part, the government passed laws prescribing a fortnight's paid holiday and the principle of the forty-hour week, and they ordered a review of some of the provisions of the Labour Code in order to facilitate the conclusion of collective agreements (for example, procedures for their compulsory extension in time or in scope were introduced).

1936 also differed from the earlier movements in that the demands had not been carefully prepared beforehand. As the strikes spread they embraced objectives that inevitably differed from one firm to another. What gave unity to these demands was the centralized negotiation that took place a couple of weeks later. Precisely the same thing was to happen in 1968. 1936 also had a strong demonstrative element: for the first time in a general strike, workplaces were occupied by the strikers. Previously strikes had always taken place outside. Was this a way of expressing hostility to the state power and a determination to conquer it? Did strikes inside the factory indicate that workers were seeking more power over their own labour?

1947: The first major strikes of this year occurred in the spring; they were supported by the Communists, after which the Communist ministers were expelled from the Ramadier government. But the largest movements began in late autumn (there were 23·3 million days lost by strikes over the whole year). There is considerable disagreement over what the objectives were. There were of course explicit demands published by the national strike committee: a 25 per cent wage increase, a minimum wage of 10,000 francs, a quarterly review of wages (this was the first time *all* the demands related to wages). But were these a cover for the real political objectives? Non-communists at the time believed so. However, the political motives ascribed to the strike were contradictory: was it a revolutionary movement intended to result in a Communist takeover of power, or was it a movement to bring about the fall of the government and a return to a tri-partite coalition including the Communists? Or was the objective more limited for the moment: merely to stop the Marshall Plan's being accepted (the Communists asserted that it would mean the enslavement of France) and so leave the way open to the development of a revolutionary situation? As it was, a strike of over three weeks – from mid-November to 9 December – was not enough to bring down the government, and the national strike committee called for a return to work. Furthermore, the strike also failed of achieving its immediate demands: the government merely promised to hold consultations with the main economic and social organizations, and to pass legislation to ensure that wages bore a reasonable relation to prices.

1968: The 1968 strikes (an estimated 150 million days lost) are so recent that it hardly seems necessary to say much about them: the demonstrative element (suggesting an alternative society, arguing for workers' self-management) was even stronger than in previous times. As in 1936, there was no programme of demands as such when the movement was launched (the concerted action of the CGT and CFDT of January 1966 had definitely run out of steam by the end of 1967); the unions formulated their precise demands only when the Grenelle negotiations opened, presenting them separately, since each organization had its own specific demand or demands (the CFDT wanting reform of structures, the CGT a sliding scale); nor were there ever very many demands. The results took the form of a statement of agreement which was in any case later thrown out by the strikers and re-negotiated separately by the various trades and then within individual firms. The chief results involved an increase in the national minimum wage and in wages as a whole, and the acceptance of union rights in all firms. The 1968 strikes also gave a stimulus to the national inter-industry negotiations which ended in agreements on employ-ment, job training and monthly salary status. There was no point at which the unions saw the situation as revolutionary: they wanted a change of government, and they said so. Hence they supported General de Gaulle's decision to hold an election for the legislature – which brought in the largest right-wing majority France has had under either the Fourth Republic or the Fifth!

We may sum up, then, by saying that a certain progression can be recognized in the mass strikes in France from 1906 to 1968. All of them presented explicit demands which tended to become more numerous and more varied as time went on. In 1906 it was the eight-hour day; by 1968 the main objective was to open negotiations. We also perceive differences in the amount of planning that went into each: 1906 was planned two years in advance; the 1920 strikes were called by all the unions at once; 1947 was launched earlier than the CGT had envisaged; 1936 and 1968 came as a surprise to the leadership of both union federations. We find differences, too, not in the fact of political objectives (which they all had) but in the nature of those objectives: it was revolution in 1906 (though only at debating level) and 1919–20; pressure on a friendly government in 1936; pressure to achieve a change of political majority in 1968; conflicting political aims in 1947. We also see differences in method: only in 1906 was recourse had to direct action: 'From 1 May 1906, we shall only work eight hours a day.' And, finally, we see differences in the results: three failures, and two successes (1936, 1968).

The 1926 General Strike in Great Britain: This had certain features in common with the French strikes of 1919 and 1920. It was the largest strike ever to have taken place in the country (over 126 million working days in 1926); it involved, as a latent demand, the whole question of the ownership of one sector of industry (the mines); it adopted not dissimilar tactics (bringing out different sectors of industry on strike one after another); it had no precisely defined political aim; it ended in serious failure; it led both to a reduction of trade union influence and to progress by the extreme left.

In 1924 the miners had gained a wage increase. In 1925 the owners took advantage of the return of the Conservatives to power to make falling exports an excuse for demanding a return to lower wages and an eight-hour day (Pelling, 1963). Stocks were too high to make a strike practicable; but the miners had the support of the T U C General Council, which asked the railwaymen and other transport workers to prevent all movement of coal. The government gave way and proposed a temporary subsidy to enable existing wages and hours to be maintained; at the same time they set up a commission to discuss the future of the mining industry. On 1 May 1926 the subsidy ran out; meanwhile, the commission's report was unfavourable to the miners. It was to be a trial of strength.

On 3 May one last attempt at negotiation failed. The strike began in several vital sectors, and then moved on to include further sectors; the level of participation was extremely high. Nevertheless after nine days the strike ended in total defeat. There were several reasons: the government had been prepared for a strike of a year, and had therefore ensured the transport of essential goods; the T U C General Council had no revolutionary orientation, and could therefore do nothing but negotiate – which they did without a single miners' representative among them; they yielded all along the line, without gaining a single concession in return. Despite accusations of treason, a return to work was decreed. The miners stayed out on strike alone till November, however, but achieved nothing.

The failure of the strike had a direct, and quite disastrous, effect on the trade union movement. It lost over half a million members, and much of its prestige. Serious dissensions arose. Above all, the 1926 débâcle enabled the government to pass the repressive Trade Disputes and Trade Union Act in 1927: this law made sympathetic strike action illegal, as well as any attempt 'to coerce the government' and any 'intimidation'; civil servants were forbidden to join any union affiliated to the T U C; finally, it reduced the income of the Labour Party by ruling that the political levy should only be paid by members who chose to 'contract in' (having formerly been paid by all unless they opted to 'contract out'). It took the Labour Party almost twenty years to get the Act repealed. The 1926 strike is the only strike in Britain ever to have had the characteristics of a general strike; the major strikes of recent years have never been on so large a scale or had such wide implications.

The aims of a go-slow

A go-slow is sabotage to the extent that it leads to slowing down production. The aims can be various; in some cases it takes the form of direct action which achieves its effect simply by taking place.

What do workers hope to get out of a go-slow? Early studies suggested that they want to establish an advantageous relationship between their work and their pay. A sensible worker will increase his output once he can be sure that by doing so he will earn more. But there can be various different reasons for working slowly: fear of overproduction, for instance, or the stepping up of management demands. Cultural norms can also explain a reluctance to produce more: workers will stop trying once they have reached the wage-level that seems adequate to their needs. The economist François Simiand, however, writing at the beginning of the century, studied the incidence of different behaviour patterns among workers and concluded that the tendency to reduce effort is less significant than the tendency to want higher earnings.

F. W. Taylor, writing in 1909, blames management for idleness on the part of workers; they invite it, he says, by the prevailing method of payment (piece-work), by overlong hours, by failing to organize work efficiently. But in theory piece-work is supposed to induce people to work their hardest. False, says Taylor. Experience shows that if workers produce more, the employer will lower the rate per piece. So, by working slowly and not letting it appear how much work he could do, the worker protects his present rate of pay. Overlong hours are the second reason for idleness: Taylor reckons that workers cannot keep up an intensive pace for ten and a half hours, and are bound to spend some time idling. Finally, workers slow down because employers make it easy for them to do so: unscientific work organization results in waste of effort on the part of the workers; they are left with nothing to do for long periods. Taylor finds it understandable that workers behave in this way when faced with managerial inefficiency; but on the other hand he explains that they are mistaken in working slowly to avoid overproduction and the dismissals and unemployment that will result. The opposite, he says, is the case: going slow results in making goods expensive and in a shrinking market which may well lead to unemployment. Taylor's was the first analysis to stress the extent to which management is responsible for time-wasting; but in so doing he sees idling by workers solely as a defensive action. Pouget, writing at the same time, describes a more offensive approach to the sabotage of reducing production. He advises workers: 'Your boss fixes your wages, so you must adapt your production to match them; if he reduces wages, you reduce production. Poor work for poor pay.' T. Lupton (1963) follows a similar line to Taylor's in blaming management for go-slow practices: he shows that they tend to happen when working conditions are not as good as they might be, in which case going slow becomes a protest, a means of drawing attention to things that hamper people from working well.

Between the wars the human-relations school highlighted a further element: going slow may be explained not only in terms of the system of payment, but also of the workers' group. The imposition of a production-ceiling is intended to prevent the kind of competition among workers that disrupts the equilibrium of interpersonal relations: it establishes and safeguards the solidarity of the group as against the employer. Anyone who infringes the norm is choosing to exclude himself from the group, and must be prepared for possible reprisals by his fellow-workers. So, in the context of human relations, the go-slow becomes a means whereby a specific group affirms its homogeneity, and the elements of resistance and defence against the employer become secondary.

More recently a number of analyses have once again emphasized the link between work and earnings. P. Rolle has studied resistance to work-timing, in other words going slow when a production target is being established. Workers put pressure on the time-and-motion officer, reduce the speed of their machines and slow down their movements or introduce additional movements they would not normally make. The aim of resisting work-timing is thus to ensure that wages remain stable by preserving the status quo, but, by screening the worker's real activity, it also enables him to keep some control over what he does – something that scientific management makes less and less possible. P. Sartin goes still further: in his view, resistance to work-timing is intended to show that a norm established by such a procedure cannot possibly be scientific: 'The imposed norms which come closest to the reality workers will accept are not those fixed by work-timing or other scientific methods, but those established by a good worker or foreman who knows from experience how long it really takes to do the job.'

The go-slow may occur not when the production norm is fixed, but afterwards, when wages are cut (Hethy and Mako, 1974). In a Hungarian plant making railway equipment, it was noted that every time the management cut the wage-rate a number of workers considerably reduced the amount of work they did. They consequently suffered a large drop in earnings, since the reduction of the piece-rate was compounded by a deliberate drop in production. What was the explanation? Why were those workers not trying to produce *more* and keep their wages the same, as all the others (who were in fact younger) did? The objective of their go-slow was to force the management to reverse its decision, so it was being used as an instrument of pressure. The workers were also drawing on their past experience: they knew that the drop in earnings would be made up in the not too far distant future – for experience had taught them that after a period of low production resulting from a go-slow, the management always raised wages, and, more important, offered a lot of very well-paid overtime. Thus this go-slow was part of a longer-term wage strategy.

But a go-slow may not always be to do with questions of wages (C. Durand, Prestat and Willener, 1972). It can be a workers' production policy geared to a specific system of production (moderate automation and a large element of workers' control over the quantity of goods produced) and payment (partly related to profits). One go-slow, in a process of hand steel-rolling, consisted in drawing out the normal break-times, stopping work early and slowing the pace of the rollers; a production ceiling was clearly established that bore no relation to what was technically possible. These workers were going slow for five reasons: to stabilize the norm and thus the level of earnings, to spare their health (the increased earnings gained by extra effort did not seem worth the strain), to preserve a certain margin of freedom for themselves, to create solidarity between successive shifts and, finally, to ensure that work done well would be properly appreciated (if the collectively determined norms were exceeded, there was a risk of accidents to the machines and a larger number of rejects).

It would seem that, given the way work systems have changed (both technically and in terms of organization) and systems of payment as well, a go-slow today will generally have different objectives from the past. Most past studies indicated that the go-slow was a response by workers to payment by results: a means of preserving present norms or getting them revised, a protest against the raising of norms, a tactic to prevent the establishment of norms by work-timing, and sometimes an adaptation to existing norms (poor work for poor pay). But with the gradual move away from payment by results and the almost total disappearance of wage-reductions, the economic dimension of the go-slow has changed somewhat: where wages are stable, a go-slow can be a direct action to get the most for one's money by doing less work for the same pay; more commonly it becomes a means of pressure for getting wages raised. In this case it is a substitute for an all-out strike.

A go-slow for objectives that are not directly economic is also a more frequent occurrence today: it is beginning to be used in disputes over mass dismissals. No longer is it the preventive measure conceived by F. W. Taylor's workers to stave off a crisis of over-production; it is the tactic of workers about to become unemployed (e.g. at Lip). Today, too, it is more often a direct action against too heavy a workload, the go-slow itself achieving the objective: the workers slow down to slacken a diabolical pace of work, to get a bit of extra rest or to increase their free time (in a case where they make a unilateral decision to cut working hours). In cutting down his workload a worker may be simply trying to reduce fatigue, but he may also be aiming to recover a certain autonomy, a certain control over his own work, which has been denied him under a scientific system of work organization.

A go-slow, finally, like the other forms of sabotage we have looked at, can take on a dimension of demonstration, of pointing to alternatives. The human-relations school point to it as a means of preserving interpersonal relationships within a group. More generally, and from a different standpoint, one can say that a collective go-slow is a means of creating group solidarity (eliminating competition between more and less competent workers, enforcing a certain homogeneity of behaviour and showing that, whatever people may think, production depends on the workers). It is a means of consolidating the group, but also a means of demonstrating opposition: workers on a go-slow stop obeying orders and observing prescribed work methods, and the authority of management is disputed and flouted. In the Lip dispute the restriction of production also played a certain evocative role: many of those involved hoped, by producing more slowly, to suggest the possibility of a different society, in which the pace of work would be more relaxed.

What results does a go-slow achieve? In the case of direct action – i.e., when a result is sought without going by way of negotiation – the objective is attained for as long as the go-slow continues, and no longer. The result is therefore temporary, being tied to the action itself (lightening the workload, not letting it be seen how much work could be done, etc.); once the go-slow ends, the situation usually reverts to what it was before. A go-slow that takes place when a norm is being established, or as a protest against its imposition, is not very effective, in that the working out of norms is now done less by direct work-timing and more by averaging out previously established times (the 'work factor' method). The temporary gains of a go-slow are sometimes ratified by negotiation, in which case it can stop without its achievements immediately disappearing. In one steelworks the production ceiling established by the workers' go-slow was agreed by the management; this might make it appear that the system of payment by results was pointless since it did not stimulate people to produce as much as they could; however, the management maintained it – not to stimulate effort but to prevent a drop in production (C. Durand, Prestat and Willener, 1972).

There may even be collective agreement to restrict production permanently, thus converting go-slow into the norm. F. W. Taylor fulminated against the unions which succeeded, for instance, in cutting down to a precise figure the number of jobs a welder could do in a day, or the number of bricks a bricklayer was allowed to handle. Such restrictive practices, laid down by the unions, still exist today in some trades such as book-printing and binding in France, and in industry as a whole in Britain. The Donovan Report, in its analysis of why the level of output per worker or per man-hour is markedly lower in Great Britain than in other countries of comparable economic development, lays great stress on poor utilization of manpower due to the restrictive work practices enshrined in collective agreements. In general it blames the refusal to take responsibility, the narrow limit set on the proportion of unskilled to skilled workers that may be taken on, too many hours of unproductive overtime, lack of mobility, acceptance by management of low standards of production, over-narrow job-description which allows of no flexibility, and the excessive length of tea-breaks and other interruptions. Such generalized slow working is obviously prejudicial to the development of the economy, and it indicates how powerful the trade unions are that they can get terms so favourable to their members embodied in collective bargaining agreements.

The aims of absenteeism

It is hard to ascertain the precise objectives of deliberate absenteeism – that is to say absence not due to illness, maternity, work accidents or leave officially granted for special occasions (family events, etc.) Indeed most research into the subject is concerned with absenteesim in general, not specifically what is known as unauthorized absenteeism. Furthermore, since their action is virtually never collective (apart from an occasional instance of imitation), absentees do not give any explicit reason for what they are doing. So, to find out what they are trying to gain by it, one must relate absenteeism-rates to the whole context of work; thus absenteeism may be considered in terms of escaping from the work situation, of getting money without working for it and of the value set on leisure.

Before looking at these three possibilities, two comments should be made. First: deliberate absentees are, in all probability, always the same people. I have two reasons for saying this. A study made at General Motors (Scotland) suggested that there is enormous disparity in individual behaviour as regards absenteeism: in that plant, extremes varied from the case of two workers who had not had a day's absence in six years to that of two who had had over 600 in the same period. On the other hand there was persistent absenteeism by individuals over a fairly long period: those who were absent a lot in one year (or other period) would be found to have been absent also in other years (or equivalent periods) (Behrend and Pocock, 1976). Secondly, deliberate absenteeism has quite different objectives when it is seen as a right from when it is seen as misconduct that disturbs the smooth running of the firm. J. M. M. Hill and E. L. Trist point out that in England absenteeism means one thing in the mines and quite another in the car industry: miners see absenteeism as a right, even a duty. It is quite simply dangerous to go down the pit when one is overtired; car workers, on the other hand, feel it necessary to apologize for staying away from work, for they share the management view that deliberate absenteeism is morally indefensible. In the first case absenteeism is directly intended to protect health; in the second, since everyone condemns it, it may have rather more various motives.

Deliberate absenteeism is primarily a rejection of the work situation: that is why it is commoner among manual workers than office-workers and managerial staff, among the unskilled than the skilled, among industrial workers than those in the service industries. Similarly, that is why there is often a link between the labour turnover rate and the rate of absenteeism. For instance, in that same General Motors study it emerged that the highest levels of absenteeism – whether in terms of the number of days missed or the number of absences overall – were always found among workers who were soon to leave rather than those who stayed.

What people are protesting against is work that is fragmented, exhausting, uninteresting and de-personalized. If one compares types of work with rates of absenteeism, one finds that absenteeism is highest when jobs have little variety, make few demands on the intelligence, offer little autonomy and not enough responsibility (Turner and Lawrence, 1965). F. Cioffi also stresses the link between absenteeism and social relationships at work. He believes that absenteeism is related to the size of the working group; workers stay away more in the larger groups in which it is hard to establish sustained relationships and anonymity is the rule. He suggests that the optimum size of a group is fifteen: that seems to produce a minimum of absences. There is further confirmation of this, from national studies made both in France and in Britain: there is more absenteeism in large plants than in small (French Ministry of Labour, INSEE, British Department of Health and Social Security). Finally, absenteeism is also influenced by the way authority is exercised in the working group: it is lower where there is a more democratic system, and when those in charge have had some management training (Argyle, Gardner and Cioffi, 1965).

In the more systematic study by P. Jardillier, we also find the foregoing factors making for absenteeism: it is higher when work is repetitive and requires major physical effort, when the hours are difficult (shift-work), when discipline is over-rigid and when a large number of workers are under a single foreman. However, there are two interesting points. First, rather than merely listing the factors, he tries to range them in order of importance: great physical effort and repetitiveness both conduce to absenteeism, but the first is a far more determining factor than the second; workers stay off work more because their job is tiring than because it is boring.* His second point has to do with the variability of the work situation: when it is unsettled (temporary transfers, having to stand in for someone else, sudden increases

*This is indirectly confirmed by the 1972 INSEE inquiry: absenteeism is highest among workers paid by results, whose work is in most cases extremely exhausting.

in the workload or the pace of work, the introduction of new machinery) there is always a steep rise in the absence-rate. Thus absenteeism becomes a rejection both of the work situation and of continual changes in it.

A series of experiments made recently, following the rise in absenteeism rates over the past few years, definitely confirmed this link between deliberate absenteeism and the work situation. Work was made more interesting, or semi-autonomous production groups were set up, and in almost every case there followed a reduction in absenteeism. The various components of the work situation seemed to combine to explain the reduction: more intersting work, changing from an authoritarian to a democratic system, reducing the production group to a more 'human' scale, extending the areas of autonomy in work.

It is clear then that the prime objective of deliberate absenteeism is to get away from unsatisfying work. It can also be a means of making the most of one's income. In recent years this latter aim has certainly become more widespread with more workers having monthly salary status: they can now stay off without any loss of wages (except in some instances when wages are cut by half for the first three days of absence). Of course, in order to benefit from this unearned income one has to show a valid excuse for not working – but what doctor would refuse to give a certificate to a weary worker? A great many employers complain that doctors are all too willing to give certificates just for the asking. However, both in France, and Britain the improvement in sickness pay systems only provided a temporary stimulus to absenteeism; the rate seems to stablilize after a time.

So the first economic objective of deliberate absenteeism is to sustain earnings without working. The UIMM inquiry into absenteeism in the metal-working industries concluded that the situation was roughly this: absences for illness increase when a strike is about to start – some workers, rather than admit to being strikers, prefer to go on receiving their wages. Thus, they win all round; they do not have to align themselves with the non-strikers, so they manage to maintain their income without working and yet without calling down upon themselves the wrath of their striking colleagues.

The second economic objective of deliberate absenteeism is to increase earnings without doing any more work. The workers who do the most overtime are also those with the highest rate of absences; their total hours worked is no lower than that of the others (Sartin, 1970). What exactly does this mean? It may be that workers who do overtime suffer greater fatigue – they cannot work at so gruelling a pace for very long, and then have to have some time off to recover. This is quite a likely explanation of the phenomenon, but it is not the only possible one. Overtime is usually paid at a higher rate than the basic working week, therefore it is financially advantageous to work fifty hours one week and thirty hours the following week, rather than forty hours both weeks – especially if sick-leave is paid, as it is today. But this economic target can only be envisaged where the firm's timetable allows of it. In this type of absenteeism it can be seen that some workers are trying to bring home more money while working the same number of hours as everyone else but distributing them differently in time.

There can be, finally, a third economic objective for absenteeism: to increase one's earnings by doing better-paid work outside the firm. Some workers purposely take time off their jobs to do casual work elsewhere. In country areas this happens during the harvest, and the wages lost are amply made up for by what is earned moonlighting. Workers with their own gardens, too, need to devote extra time to them at certain seasons; in this case the wages lost are eventually recovered in kind, in garden produce. Temporary work outside one's job thus contributes to increase absenteeism. That this is so has sometimes been denied (Jardillier, 1962). Surely, it is said, workers who do two jobs at once (one regular job, one moonlighting) have every reason to be punctilious: they are only doing the extra work because they have considerable financial responsibilities, so it is hardly in their interest to stay off work; they would be more likely to turn up regularly and work without a break. This, though true in the early sixties, is certainly less true today, since people are now paid for time off work as long as they have a theoretically valid excuse. A worker has everything to gain by staying away to work unofficially, especially in his own home.

Finally, in addition to being a rejection of a work situation and a means of increasing earnings, absenteeism also relates to the value set on leisure time and activities. Objectives in this third category are a logical consequence of the first: by staying off work one is rejecting work in order to replace it with something else. It may be just to enjoy oneself, to regain the control of one's own time that is lost in the factory, to cut down working time. In other words absenteeism may envisage a different way of filling one's time. Some instances of absenteeism clearly belong in this category: staying off work the day after pay-day (especially when wages are paid in cash) gives workers some free time to spend the money they have earned. Then there is staying away the day after a bank holiday – workers prolonging their festivities or sneaking in an extra day's holiday. Employers have always tried to fight against this form of absenteeism; for instance, they sometimes make working the days before and after the holiday a condition for paying any compensation for the day not worked. But whatever they do a lot of workers still treat themselves to the extra day, especially if it links up with a weekend.

Absenteeism for pleasure is also characteristic of certain categories of workers: immigrant workers who go home for holidays will often stay away till their money runs out; people without family responsibilities prefer to spend all that they earn at once, rather than saving it up for a rainy day. (Here too, changes seem to be taking place: in the early sixties there was little absenteeism among unmarried girls (Jardillier, 1962), whereas the UIMM inquiry has shown that today youth and unmarried status are both positive factors in absenteeism.) Finally, married women who only work to supplement the family income will often stop working when they feel they have earned enough; they still set a higher value on non-working time, and want as much of it as possible.

Absenteeism, considered as a means whereby a worker whose time is normally not his own regains control of his own time, can also be a precautionary measure: if the workload is too heavy one takes a break for health reasons. By staying off work *now* one is preventing what seems almost certain to happen otherwise – having to stay off sick later on. In this sense, too, absenteeism is a re-possession of one's own time: rather than being obliged to spend time being ill, one makes one's own decision by taking some rest as a preventive. Such, I am sure, is the perspective in which one should interpret the statistics of the French National Insurance Fund which show that from 1969 to 1973 absences of under three months rose by 21·3 per cent, whereas those of over three months went down by over 11 per cent.

Deliberate absenteeism, whether it means rejection of work, a way of earning money effortlessly or just a wish to enjoy one-self, is seldom acknowledged explicitly as such – after all, un-authorized absence can lead to disciplinary action or even dismissal. Only in private conversation will absentees who are neither sick nor hurt admit that they use their rights to sickness pay in just the same way as they take their normal paid holidays. Thus, deliberate absenteeism is a clandestine form of action. It is direct action, since the result is achieved simply by taking the action; it is always successful for people prepared to take the risk. But returning to work means returning to the same situation as before, therefore deliberate absenteeism only produces a temporary success. However, it can have certain indirect con-sequences: it is a warning signal for the employer, and may lead to a reorganization of work (cf. Chapter 5 below).

One case: the sabotage at Lip

On 21 April 1973 the president of the Board of Directors of Lip resigned; two temporary directors were appointed, and let it be known that 'staff cuts would be necessary'. The Lip workers thereupon instituted the first form of sabotage: they slowed down production. On 12 June the temporary directors announced that wages would no longer be paid. This was equivalent to announc-ing general dismissals, so a second form of sabotage was instituted in response: the theft of watches (in three stages – the theft itself, the sale of what was stolen, and the use of the money as strike pay). From 13 June a third form of action went into effect: production was started again. This was not sabotage in the normal sense, but it was so indirectly, since the work was done at a very slow pace and the goods produced were not sold in the regular market. The fourth and final form of sabotage was the total shutdown of production from October 1973 to the end of January 1974, even though a solution for re-starting the firm had been proposed (the premises offered by the local authority were systematically dismantled by the workers). Let us consider successively the aims of these four forms of direct or indirect sabotage, for no dispute in France in recent years has included so many different forms of sabotage at once, and the most varied explanations have been put forward (de Virieu, 1973; Piaget, 1973; Lourau, 1974; Barou, 1975).

On 23 April 1973 the temporary directors made a general announcement: 'Anything may happen. We cannot guarantee jobs, nor can we guarantee not to close down some departments. Staff cuts will be necessary.' The workers responded to this threat by their first type of action: a production go-slow. It spread first to the heavy machinery and armaments sections – by the end of May these were only working at 10 to 20 per cent of capacity. It took longer for the slowing-down process to reach the watch section. This was still working at 50 per cent of capacity by the end of May, but went down to 30 per cent early in June. The workers refused to accept discipline, reduced the speed of operations, left their benches without permission, held meetings during working hours. What was this action intended to achieve? No explicit demand was linked to it; the firm had not yet laid off a single worker; the go-slow was intended simply to find out what the employers were proposing to do. Yet everyone felt that it had struck home. So the go-slow, though not formulating demands, had several aims: to harden the workforce by creating a clear situation of struggle; to establish the workers in an offensive position; to prepare for open war and have their demands ready. It was during those May meetings on the shopfloor that the three objectives were hammered out that were retained until January 1974: no lay-offs, no closures in any of the three sections of production, and the retention of all existing benefits. Finally, the go-slow aimed to conserve strength for the future: the management threatened to pay only the hours actually worked, but the threat was not carried out – everyone received their full wages throughout May. In short, this go-slow was not making any explicit demand; it was not trying to reduce production to save jobs, by taking longer to fill orders, nor was it seeking any improvement in working conditions. It was a preparation for war.

On 13 June 57,000 watches – some complete, some waiting to be assembled – were taken from stock: ten million francs' worth. This 'theft' was first and foremost an act of self-defence: the directors said that wages would no longer be paid and there would be no severance or redundancy pay, so the watches were taken to be used as cash. The workers stole to be sure of getting what was owed to them. The second aim was strategic: the theft took place immediately after the police had intervened to release the temporary directors locked up by the workers; this was a way of keeping the intitiative, strengthening the workers' will to fight, and making the public aware of what was going on. The third objective of the theft was protest: it was an illegal act, but it followed a great many acts by management that were also illegal (the failure to take any proceedings against the Lip directors, the refusal to pay the wages owed to the workers though managerial staff were still being paid, failure to consult the works committee and the Factory Inspector, disregard of the National Employment Agreements). The illegality of the workers was therefore a protest against the illegality of the employers. Finally, the sale of the stolen watches and the use of the money for strike pay reveals the final aim: to hang on – which could only be done if people were paid enough to survive. So the strike pay became a form of direct action: the workers no longer demanded concessions – they took.

As to what they hoped to gain by starting up production again, there is rather more disagreement. The CGT, for instance, conducted an analysis which led them to conclude that it was done for the same reasons as the sale of the stolen watches: they produced watches to sell, in self-defence, to sustain their fighting spirit and to ensure a subsistence wage. But in my view this is an over-simplification. The workers involved set about the work in a quite different way. Not everyone worked – only fifty out of 1,300 were actually occupied on the assembly lines. Everything about the work situation was changed – the hours worked, which worker was assigned to which position, the nature of the jobs, the hierarchical structure and the way decisions were made, the flow of work. The only thing that was unchanged was the retention of wage differentials: a proposal to equalize wages when the first pay-out was made was rejected by everyone.

The group ruled supreme: every morning it assembled, and decided which models would be produced, in what numbers and at what rate. Thus workers' autonomy took on new meaning. Since the role of the hierarchy was taken over by the group, there was no need for anyone to be in charge, and such foremen as took part in the action simply worked their machines like everyone else. The pace of production was slowed down: the assembly line usually produced 2,500 watches per day, whereas the target set by the group of volunteers was 800, though in practice they produced between 1,100 and 1,200. In fact they continued to work quite fast ('knowing it was for our own benefit, we went twice as fast'), and it was only the fact of cutting the working day to four or five hours that caused production to drop. This, then, was worker freedom – but did that make the work itself more interesting? The workers in fact now controlled the machines; some jobs could be restructured, others not; the same processes had to be carried out, but it was arranged that people should move from place to place on the line. Altering the work set-up was a direct action that produced immediate changes. What was its objective? To the CFDT there could be no two opinions about that: the Lip workers were trying to suggest the possibility of a different society, to show that employers were not indispensable, that workers could manage and organize themselves, that a new style of less hierarchical work relationships was possible – in short, to demonstrate the credibility of workers' control. They certainly started up production again for a practical purpose (to sell watches), but more important was the demonstrative element (to suggest a different kind of work organization).

R. Lourau (1974) draws different conclusions from the fact that the Lip workers were divided into those who carried on production and those who simply struck and did no work. The first, he says, were anxious to show by their behaviour that they wanted to save the firm; they demonstrated and expressed an ideology of work, that consciousness of their own skill, so dear to the aristocracy of labour, which consisted in proving that they could work without managerial supervision. The others were expressing an ideology of striking for its own sake; by not working they were protesting against industry in general, its feudal structure, its idealization of productivity and its managerial class. And Lourau believes they were right: they represented a hesitant recrudescence of the ideology of non-work so long repressed by the traditions of the labour movement. I think this interpretation goes too far: it minimizes the importance of the reorganization of work by those who started up production, and maximizes the importance of the ideology of non-work in this dispute. I find none of the evidence adduced convincing. Those who worked for the fifty-six days before the factory was occupied by the police also supported a certain kind of non-work by cutting down working hours. There was certainly no such clear-cut opposition between the two camps.

The fourth phase of the sabotage at Lip was the continuance of the strike after the negotiations of October 1973 broke down. The workers were to sustain for a further three months the three explicit demands they had begun with: no dismissals, no cutting down on any of the three sections of production and the retention of all existing benefits. On 8 January 1974 they sabotaged the disused factory loaned by the municipality, where M. Arbel had been authorized to re-establish the civil and military heavy-machinery sections. 'If Arbel wants to wreck us, we'll wreck his plant.' The workers formed a line; tiles were passed from hand to hand, doors and windows were removed; and they sang (to the tune of 'Alouette'):

Arbelette, vilaine Arbelette, Arbelette, nous te plumerons.
Nous te plumerons les portes, nous te plumerons les portes,
Et les fenêtres,
Et les tuiles,
Et les chiottes,
Et la pointeuse,
Et les volets ...

On 29 January, by the Dole formula of agreement, they achieved almost total satisfaction on the first two points; in relating to existing benefits the situation was more doubtful.

The work stoppage continued for three months after production could have begun again in November. Was the satisfaction of the three explicit demands all that was envisaged? Obviously not. From the moment the stocks of watches were seized in June, the Lip strike became a beacon. Even in 1968 workers had never dared to expropriate manufactured goods; this time they did. Public opinion was on their side, and from early summer the authorities tried to set up a plan for re-launching the industry. Lip thus took on a political aspect, bringing the workers' movement as a whole into confrontation with the government. The Lip workers had become an example, and they could not afford to lose: their defeat would mean the defeat of the whole trade union movement, whereas their victory would have tremendous repercussions and greatly strengthen the hand of the unions. That was the first political fact. The second was that a breach had been made in capitalist legality: to contest dismissals was an attack on the employer's property rights, his right unilaterally to break work contracts; it demonstrated how inadequately workers were protected in their employment; and at the same time it was a campaign for new labour laws which would no longer allow managements to dismiss workers without warning. In this respect the Lip strike was to lead to several positive changes in French law: the law of 27 December 1973 making it obligatory to pay all wages and give compensation for a dismissal was a direct result of it. And it also led to the various revisions in 1974 of national agreements on job security and redundancy payments.

Finally, the persistence of the Lip workers during the last three months of the dispute was due to their wish to see more vigorous methods of action used extensively in employment disputes. If they lost, then workers dismissed in future would be tempted to accept whatever happened fatalistically, whereas if they won it would make it easier for others to take an offensive stand against mass redundancies. They did win, and since then disputes whose main demand has been to save jobs have been conducted quite differently – lasting longer, and with strikers more readily resorting to illegal forms of action.

The various forms of sabotage perpetrated by the Lip workers (the go-slow, the sale of watches, the continuance of production, the last-ditch strike) were aimed at a multitude of objectives – the entire range of possible objectives described at the beginning of this chapter. Their strike envisaged the achievement of certain practical demands, some explicit (no dismissals, no closures, no loss of existing benefits), some implicit (contesting the absolute authority of management, objecting to a legal system that allowed employers to dismiss workers when it suited them). It also envisaged certain practical political aims (making the government admit defeat, getting the law on employment reformed, strengthening the workers' movement). And it also had a variety of demonstrative aims: the starting up of production, especially, was concrete evidence of the possibility of other forms of work organization. Finally, the Lip strike was also an example – of how to wage an offensive battle against mass lay-offs (the sale of watches and distribution of the proceeds had a decisive influence, and became a model for other strikes).

Summary

There can be many motives for sabotage (destructive sabotage, sabotage-strikes, go-slows and absenteeism): various immediate demands, political aims, to demonstrate opposition to an enemy or to display one's own strength. As compared with other forms of industrial action, such as switching off the machinery or presenting demands via a representative, sabotage certainly has a far wider variety of aims (in fact a single act of sabotage alone can have a number of different objectives), is more expressive, can achieve its results by direct action, thus bypassing negotiation, and is at least equally effective. It is those aims and results that have determined the theories produced throughout the history of the workers' movement.

3 Theories: For and Against Sabotage

Sabotage, as we have seen, may have one objective or several: it can be used to back up demands, to initiate political change or to express a generalized opposition. And theories will be determined partly in relation to those objectives. There are two main traditions in France, one hostile to any sabotage that destroys machinery or pointlessly reduces production, the other regarding such practices as quite legitimate. The first makes the political objective the overriding one in every struggle: a particular dispute must not be allowed to hinder the coming of socialism, and since machine-breaking is an obstacle to changing society, because it divides the workers, it must therefore be condemned. The second is concerned with immediate changes, and favours all forms of action that demonstrate opposition to the management; it does not want to wait for some future date to change working conditions; any sabotage that leads to an immediate improvement is legitimate.

The first line of thought is represented by Marxist tradition. Back in 1845 Engels declared that sabotage was inappropriate, that it could only be a hindrance to the wider political struggle for the conquest of state power. The C G T has aligned itself with that tradition since just after the First World War, and, except during the last war, it has continuously preached respect for the machine. The second line belongs to the anarchist tradition that grew up at the end of the last century. The pre-1914 C G T, which was syndicalist and revolutionary, supported that tradition, voting in favour of sabotage at its congresses – in fact, many of its leaders were former anarchists. A number of Maoist groups in industry today can be seen as fitting into this tradition, too, though some of them in fact see sabotage as a means towards achieving a total transformation of society. The present-day C F D T sometimes takes this tradition as inspiration for certain forms of struggle, but its political strategy leads it to ally itself with the anti-sabotage line and so condemn any other.

I shall start this chapter, therefore, by contrasting the two: the theory defined by Engels, and the far more fluid theory of anarchism. I then turn to a chronological study, considering the positions adopted by the revolutionary-syndicalist C G T before 1914, and those adopted by the C G T from 1918 to 1968. Finally, I turn to present-day trade union theory, as it emerges from various specific events and then from an overall view. The chapter concludes with an analysis of the theory of certain French Maoist groups.

Two opposing theories: Marxism versus anarchism

In *The Condition of the Working-Class in England in 1844* Engels deals with sabotage and strikes. He judges them in relation to what should be the major objective of the working class – the ending of bourgeois domination and the elimination of wage-labour – which can only be effected by the conquest of state power after a revolutionary struggle (which may or may not be violent). Whatever serves to prepare the proletariat for that political struggle is legitimate; anything that impedes their advance towards it is taboo. Destructive sabotage is condemned; strikes are allowed, but only under certain conditions.

Engels explains that 'the revolt of the workers ... has passed through several phases': theft and crime, machine-breaking, trade union organization and strikes, the struggle for state power. The earlier forms of revolt must be replaced with better ones.

The revolt of the workers began soon after the first industrial development ... The earliest, crudest, and least fruitful form of this rebellion was that of crime. The working-man lived in poverty and want, and saw that others were better off than he. It was not clear to his mind why he, who did more for society than the rich idler, should be the one to suffer under these conditions. Want conquered his inherited respect for the sacredness of property, and he stole ... The workers soon realised that crime did not help matters. The criminal could protest against the existing order of society only singly, as one individual; the whole might of society was brought to bear upon each criminal, and crushed him with immense superiority. Besides, theft was the most primitive form of protest, and for this reason, if for no other, it never became the universal expression of the public opinion of the working-men, however much they might approve of it in silence.

Engels also found destructive sabotage inappropriate, for similar reasons:

As a class, they first manifested opposition to the bourgeoisie when they resisted the introduction of machinery at the very beginning of the industrial period. The first inventors, Arkwright and others, were persecuted in this way, and their machines destroyed. Later, there took place a number of revolts against machinery ... This form of opposition also was isolated, restricted to certain localities, and directed against one feature only of our present social arrangements. When the momentary end was attained, the whole weight of social power fell upon the unprotected evil-doers and punished them to its heart's content, while the machinery was introduced none the less.

Free right of association was recognized in England in 1824. The trade unions advanced rapidly, and organized campaigns for raising wages, or against lowering them. Did Engels see this form of opposition to the bourgeoisie as any more worthwhile? Yes and no. Strikes are justified, but they can never overthrow the power of the bourgeoisie.

The history of these Unions is a long series of defeats of the working-men, interrupted by a few isolated victories. All these efforts naturally cannot alter the economic law according to which wages are determined by the relation between supply and demand in the labour market. Hence the Unions remain powerless against all *great* forces which influence this relation.

However, the unions and the strikes they actuate are not entirely valueless:

The active resistance of the English working-men has its effect in holding the money greed of the bourgeoisie within certain limits, and keeping alive the opposition of the workers to the social omnipotence of the bourgeoisie ... But what gives these Unions and the strikes arising from them their real importance is this, that they are the first attempt of the workers to abolish competition. They imply the recognition of the fact that the supremacy of the bourgeoisie is based wholly upon the competition of the workers among themselves; i.e., upon their want of cohesion.

Here we find Engels already giving reasons for condemning various forms of action, arguments that were to be taken up later by Marxist organizations and especially by the trade unions. He affirms the primacy of the political struggle for the conquest of state power; it takes precedence over the struggle for immediate gains, and any form of action that hinders the advance of the political struggle, whatever the immediate gains, is to be rejected – theft and destructive sabotage are condemned, and the strike, though necessary, does not go far enough. These Marxist positions (described as authoritarian) were to be confronted, within the First International set up in 1864, by another, so-called anti-authoritarian, line of thinking, a line that was to inspire the methods of the anarchist movement and the French syndicalist movement of the late nineteenth and early twentieth centuries. According to this theory, sabotage, theft and strikes – especially revolutionary general strikes – are absolutely legitimate forms of action and quite self-sufficient.

Some tendencies within the anarchist movement support such measures as theft, arson, sabotage and other direct action. In contrast to the Marxists, anarchists do not believe that

the revolution will be a set battle fought out by daylight, but a guerrilla war waged in secrecy, by individual actions, and on a solely economic plane. They certainly make no claim that the social problem can be solved by such means, but they believe that there should be acts of this kind to focus the attention of the exploited on their real enemies – the employers – and to prevent workers' straying onto the political field until the time of the revolution comes [quoted in Maitron, 1975].

Some anarchist groups would permit theft or expropriation by individuals. In 1885 and 1887 this was declared legitimate in their newspaper, *Le Révolté*:

The workers who, during a strike, take possession of workshops and settle in them after having driven their exploiters out, the hungry man who is penniless, and goes into shops to take what he needs – whether with others or alone – these are actions we can feel solidarity with, for they are the actions of genuine rebels ... In creating man, nature gave him the right to exist, and it is his duty to exercise that right fully. Therefore, if society does not give him what he needs to live, a human being can legitimately take what he needs from wherever there is an excess.

On the other hand, when the international anarchist meeting in Paris in July 1889 debated the subject of theft, it came to no clear unanimous conclusion. When there was a return to illegal activities after 1900, with armed robberies that sometimes led to murder, these too aroused considerable controversy in the anarchist movement.

Anarchist propaganda was active among the working class. The anarchists took the occasion of May Day demonstrations – especially 1 May 1890 – to jeer at those who marched peacefully in the streets. At Vienne in 1890 Tennevin, an anarchist propagandist, made a highly incendiary speech:

On the first of May, workers must go to their employers' homes and take all their possessions, and if they put up any resistance, then their heads should be broken. Steal, take everything, burn if necessary, kill the employers. It is your right, for your employer is exploiting you. Taking from him is not stealing; it is simply taking back what is yours by right ... Workers must break the machines and set fire to the factories! [Quoted in Maitron, 1975.]

When the day came, all that happened was that a few demonstrators attacked a cloth warehouse, seized 43 metres of material and divided it among themselves. Despite their faith in propaganda of the deed, the anarchists sometimes forgot the deed and put all their energy into the propaganda.

The anarchists were also behind the direct-action methods later taken up by the French trade union movement in the pre-1914 period. In February 1875 Adhemar Schwitzguebel, in the *Bulletin de la fédération jurassienne*, urged direct action to get working hours reduced – in other words, a form of go-slow. He clearly had no faith in 'politics'.

For workers who want working hours restricted, a federal law will not really improve matters. When they think the time is ripe to introduce this reform in a particular trade, they will be in a position to do it through the activity of resistance groups. Rather than begging the Confederation to make a decree obliging employers to limit working hours, the shop itself will enforce this reform on the employers directly. Consequently, instead of a legal formula which may well remain a dead letter, it will be transformed into economic reality by the direct initiative of the workers [quoted in Maitron, 1975].

The pre-1914 revolutionary-syndicalist CGT: in favour of sabotage

The Marxist and anarchist lines were soon to be in confrontation in the French trade union movement, which was gradually reconstructed after the repression of the Commune in 1871. From 1894 on the tendency known as anarcho-syndicalism or revolutionary syndicalism came to be very significant. This type of syndicalism spread to the United States with the setting up of the Industrial Workers of the World in 1905. Its theory was definitely anti-Marxist, rejecting the idea that the role of the Party was more important than that of the trade union. Revolutionary syndicalism borrowed certain forms of action from ånarchism; it also learnt from it a mistrust of electoralist politics. but it nevertheless worked out a theory of how a socialist society would be achieved by means of a revolutionary general strike directed by the trade union organization.

The best formulation of revolutionary syndicalist theory was produced by the Amiens Congress in 1906. Objectives and forms of action were defined very clearly: syndicalism has 'a twofold task: a day-to-day task, and a task for the future'.

In the work of making day-to-day demands, it aims to coordinate workers' efforts, to increase the well-being of the workers by achieving immediate improvements ... but this is only one side of its job; it is working for the full emancipation that can only be achieved by expropriation of capital; it envisages the general strike as the means of action, and believes that the trade union that is today a resistance group will, in the future, be the production and distribution group, the basis of social reorganization.

Sabotage was recognized as a useful form of action to assist 'the work of making day-to-day demands' at the 1897 congress (the

third C G T congress). Delesalle got the congress to adopt –
unanimously and with cheers – a report recommending boycotts
and sabotage. At the Paris congress in 1900 a motion on sabotage
received 117 votes in favour and 76 against. Pouget became the
most ardent supporter of this method: it was legitimate because
effective, and useful in pedagogical terms because it accustomed
the worker to become self-reliant.

We all know that the exploiter normally chooses his moment to
tighten the bonds of our servitude – the moment when it is hardest for
us to resist his encroachments by a partial strike (which is the only means
used up to now). Sabotage totally changes the picture: workers can
resist; they are no longer simply at the mercy of capital . . . We have an
effective weapon of resistance which will enable us to stand up to the
exploitation we are subjected to until the time comes when workers
have the power to free themselves completely· . . . Continuous and
unremitting sabotage has the advantage of developing a sense of
initiative, getting people used to acting for themselves and arousing a
combative spirit.

'Sabotage' primarily means working slowly and lowering the
quality of what is produced; should it also be used on machines?
Pouget says yes, but the way he phrases his statement suggests
that he finds himself faced with a contradiction on the point:

The worker will only respect machinery on the day when it becomes
his friend, shortening his work, rather than as today his enemy, taking
away jobs, killing workers. Workers have no systematic will to destroy
apart from their concern with the aim of such destruction: if workers
attack machinery, it is not for fun or because they have nothing better
to do, but because they are driven by imperious necessity.

Despite the fact that some trade union leaders believe in it,
machine-breaking is rare. The reverse is commoner: the machine
is now being glorified; the aim is to get possession of the machines
and then wonders will happen. 'The revolution will come by way
of industrial advance. Thus the alliance between the workers'
movement and economic growth is sealed for a long time to
come' (Perrot, 1973).

The general strike should make it possible to achieve the other
task of syndicalism: 'the full emancipation of the workers by

the abolition of wage-labour and the employing class'. The propaganda committee set up at the 1906 congress envisaged its taking place in the following stages (cf. Brecy, 1969): (1) a general strike by members of certain specified trades, comparable to preliminary manoeuvres; (2) stoppages everywhere on an agreed date, or major manoeuvres; (3) general and complete stoppage, whereby the proletariat are in open war with capitalist society; (4) general strike, revolution. How did they see the general strike? Its early proponents had great faith in simply doing nothing: all work would stop at once, and the bourgeoisie would collapse. Fernand Pelloutier, the syndicalist leader, still believed in this painless revolution: the general strike was revolutionary, but it was non-violent and legal, since it was based on the right to strike and the legality of trade unions. V. Griffuelhes, the C G T leader, considered in 1904 that the general strike would quite probably be violent: 'The general strike is not just a matter of workers' stopping their activity; it also means seizing the social wealth produced by the different groups of workers, in this case the trade unions, for the benefit of everyone. Whether this general strike, or revolution, will be violent or not depends on the resistance it meets with' (Brecy, 1969). As war drew nearer, the revolutionary strike and the destructive sabotage that would go with it came to be envisaged in greater detail. In November 1912 the C G T held a special congress in Paris, to consider the single question of 'Organizing resistance to war'. There was a pamphlet distributed by an anarchist leader which suggested measures for preventing mobilization: a rising by the trade unions and a general strike, devising and making known ways of sabotaging communications, destroying printing presses to prevent harm from being done by the bourgeois press, the refusal of the trade unions to obey orders to mobilize, and attacks on the most vulnerable points of the nation's defence by groups of reliable union members. Of these various measures, the congress adopted the sabotage of communications and the refusal to obey mobilization orders. On the day war was declared all those who were called up were to go to union headquarters to be briefed about the general strike. In 1912, also, there appeared a red booklet which the C G T leaders had combined to write. It gave detailed descriptions of ways in which the various sectors of national activity could be hampered during the call-up: telephone and telegraph communications could be broken once one knew which were the key points, gas and electricity supply-lines could be blown up, transformers set on fire, the metro stopped, cars put out of action, canal-locks stopped from working, mines flooded, railway bridges blown up and rails damaged so that engines would break down (cf. Becker, 1973).

The CGT leaders tried to help people imagine the revolution that would result from a general strike. For instance, in *Comment nous ferons la révolution*, Pouget predicts two phases: first the spread of the strike, then the re-establishment of production. During the first there may be destructive sabotage. A building strike has lasted for two weeks, and there have been meetings, rioting, even deaths. Then the strike by specific trades turns into a general strike, and there is no *Métro* any more; the rails are unbolted and the dynamos tampered with. There is no bread in the bakeries because the ovens are unusable. There is no electricity, the electrical workers having sabotaged that. The railways have stopped because cement has been poured into the points. Trade Union leaders make speeches to the effect that the strike will go on until the government gives way. Victory soon follows, as troops fraternize with workers. Production then starts again, with the trade unions in charge, having expropriated the capitalists.

Nor was it only the trade union movement that advocated a general strike. Other theorists also spoke in favour of it: Georges Sorel wrote his *Réflexions sur la violence* in 1908, in which he suggests that the general strike is a myth that can mobilize the energies of the proletariat and consequently, therefore, of the bourgeoisie as well, quite independently of whether it ever actually happens. Capitalist society, he says, is going downhill, and it is pointless for socialist politicians to recommend peace and good will and seek to get into positions of power: they will merely be preserving a state in which nothing has changed as far as the workers are concerned. This, says Sorel, is altogether the wrong tack. The myth of the general strike, whereby the pro-

letariat declares its readiness to take over from the bourgeoisie.
must change the situation. It must accentuate class divisions,
Capitalism

> will abandon its vision of social harmony and return to its essential
> nature as the creator of goods, of productive forces ... The bourgeoisie
> and the proletariat will each be obliged to muster all its forces and set
> them against the other; the more fervently capitalist the bourgeoisie,
> the more warlike and confident in its revolutionary force the prole-
> tariat, the more certain the movement [Sorel, 1908].

The 'movement' is towards the maximum development of the
forces of production. In other words, the myth of the general
strike introduces a kind of competitiveness over productivity
as between the proletariat and the bourgeoisie: the bourgeoisie,
to stave off this strike that will dispossess them, have to go all
out to safeguard economic development, while the proletariat, so
as to be ready to take command, must foster a new mentality of
productivity which can only have an immediately beneficial
effect on production. 'The idea of the general strike produces in
everyone a positively heroic state of mind, with everyone strain-
ing every nerve to create conditions that will result in a fantastic-
ally progressive and freely functioning industry'. And if one day
the general strike actually occurs (which, to Sorel, is not what
matters; the myth is more important than the reality), then the
proletariat, having by now developed a mentality of productivity,
will prove no disappointment: all their creative energies will be
free, and they will produce magnificently.

However, the French trade union movement, much as it
wanted a revolutionary general strike, proved unable to launch
one. The eight-hour general strike of 1906 was not fully observed
and never had the character of a strike of expropriation; nor did
the 1909 postal strike or the 1910 railway strike. Similarly, when
war was declared in August 1914 the C G T was unable to
launch a general strike – despite all the motions passed in its
congresses and all the handbooks distributed to inform members
of detailed practical steps to be taken to sabotage the war effort.
The opposite happened: the C G T hastened to join Poincaré's
union sacrée.

Before 1914 the trade union movement had given official and majority support to such forms of action as the destruction of machinery and goods, go-slows and boycotts; above all, it wanted to launch a general strike of expropriation. Clearly, then, the theory was unable to produce the situation it recommended as the right one: there was little sabotage and less slow working, and strikes were neither general nor revolutionary. One can point to a number of different reasons for this discrepancy between theory and reality: the trade union movement was not firmly established, was badly organized and not sufficiently centralized, there was repression by government and management, the weight of the left-wing parties and then the S F I O (the Socialist Party) favoured giving priority to the struggle for political power, and under the double influence of the bourgeoisie and Marxism the workers had too much respect for their tools.

However, the larger part of the trade union movement had, in the twenty years prior to 1914, advocated forms of action which can be generally classified as sabotage. Henceforth it was to recommend them only in exceptional circumstances.

1918 to 1968: the C G T against sabotage

Paradoxically, it was when the majority of the C G T deliberately opted for a reformist approach – seeking social intervention by the state, nationalization, a social and economic council, worker-representation in industry – that the great strikes of 1919-20 began. As we have seen, the C G T leadership was largely responsible for their failure. After the 1921 split the C G T rejected violent forms of action. The Communist C G T U sometimes admitted the possibility. In *La Stratégie des grèves* (1926), Vassart wrote: 'No class war can be honourable or legal; still less can it be peaceful. In the struggle between capital and labour, all means are good and all must be tried' (quoted in Lefranc, 1969).

By the time of the 1936 strikes, the C G T was reunified, and could congratulate itself on the calm that prevailed in the factories. At Renault the doors were barricaded in case of any possible attack by the police. There were one or two groups from the Fourth International who wanted to destroy everything, but they were made to see reason. In fact it was the other way round: the machines were oiled by the workers, and everything was in perfect order, not even a scrap of paper on the floor. There was a group in every workshop whose job was to clean and service the machines [R. Durand, 1971].

When the war came the CGT had come full circle: the pre-1914 CGT had called for sabotage to prevent mobilization when the First World War was declared, in a spirit of anti-patriotism ('proletarians have no country'). The CGT of the forties called for sabotage during the war, in the opposite spirit – its aim was the patriotic one of liberating the country. Not merely were some forms of sabotage legitimate: they were desirable. In a special number of *La Vie ouvrière* (CGT) in August 1943 there was a call to the railwaymen: 'Refuse to drive German trains; see who can do most to paralyse rail traffic; we want to see massive destruction of engines and carriages, of points, bridges, tunnels and rails' (quoted in Jacquet, 1967). In 1944 the Paris liberation committee, with the CGT militant Tollet presiding, called for a proliferation of go-slows, authorized theft in certain instances ('Electricity workers, help the population to fiddle their meters; current used by the people is current taken from the enemy') and called upon everyone to rise up and liberate Paris. Their call to action was a call for sabotage of every kind:

There must be no planes, no engines, no weapons for the Germans to use against France and her allies. No locomotives in running order, no strategic road left un-sabotaged, no grain of wheat, no animal to be requisitioned. We must not leave our oppressors a single cutting tool, a single thinking brain, a single running vehicle, a single threshing-machine that works. Sabotage machinery and production; blow up roads and canals and locks; destroy everything the enemy can use! [Quoted in Denis, 1963.]

All this represents no small change from the pre-war CGT line. But it can be explained partly by the objectives normally envisaged by sabotage, which the CGT authorized (as explained in the preceding chapter), and partly by the wish to demonstrate an exemplary patriotism which could pay political dividends after the Liberation. In this, it met with considerable success.

After the first post-Liberation election, there were several Communist ministers in the government. The C G T's attitude now changed diametrically: during the war production had to be slowed down and if necessary sabotaged; now any activity to slow down productivity was violently condemned. The CGT and the Communist Party joined in the battle for production – of coal, in particular. In July 1945 Maurice Thorez spoke to the miners, enjoining on them the single duty: produce more. Absenteeism must be cut down by making it harder to get medical certificates, and slow working must be stopped: 'It is much to be regretted that, in our Communist stronghold, the miners have not yet become aware of the enormous responsibility that rests upon them.' The moral decline among young people must also be reversed: 'They must make a great effort to learn to value work and see in it the condition for their personal liberation. The lazy and unenthusiastic will never be good Communists or good revolutionaries' (quoted in Barou, 1975). However, with the departure of the Communists from the government in May 1947, the C G T did another about-face: it now gave unhesitating support to the major strikes that brought production to a halt at the end of 1947 and the end of 1948. While there were Communists in the government the C G T hoped to win considerable social gains by demonstrating its fitness to lead the workers in the battle for production; later the same arguments did not apply.

The union federations – the C G T and *a fortiori* the C F T C – remained steadily hostile to any form of action that failed to respect the machinery of production. This applied to the electricity workers in the mid-sixties: each time there was a nation-wide strike, the power cuts were subject to discussion between the management of each power station and the unions. The management in each case, under pressure from the government, wanted to keep the production minimum as high as possible, and based their arguments on technical limitations; the unions, to ensure that supplies were not going to privileged customers, sought to reduce it to the utmost. In the end a compromise was always reached. And no equipment was ever damaged. But one day a group of workers disputed the compromise and threatened a stay-at-home strike, rather than staying at work to ensure the maintenance of the equipment – after which things were quite different. This threat of a destructive strike was fiercely opposed by the various trade union federations, which sent numbers of representatives to reason with the workers in the name of respect for the machinery of production. In 1968 their attitude was generally the same. (Barrier, 1975).

Present-day trade union theory

However, the 1968 strikes introduced a certain change in attitudes. This was especially evident in the C F D T. But before trying to sum up the movement of ideas in this area in the C G T and the C F D T and to understand the underlying reasons, it is worth trying to analyse their present-day attitudes (as illustrated in various concrete instances) towards respect for the machinery of production and the commodity produced, towards types of strike action intended to cut down production or bring it to a stop, towards go-slows, the expropriation of goods and absenteeism.

Respect for the machinery of production

The pre-1914 revolutionary syndicalist C G T officially advocated the sabotaging of goods, and accepted the sabotaging of machinery; it took exactly the same stand during the last war. But these two periods apart, the C G T has always been an ardent defender of respect for machinery, even during 1968, and since then as well. Today the C F D T occasionally supports strikers who refuse to operate safety services, but this would have been unthinkable before 1968.

During the 1968 strikes both the C G T and the C F D T approved of the occupation of factories, since that never involved any damage to the machinery of production. The C G T congratulated itself on 'the tremendous spirit of responsibility, the coolness and the great maturity of its militants'.

Everyone admits that during the three or four weeks' strike and occupation machines, complex installations, in fact all the means of production, have been conscientiously looked after by the workers on strike; safety has been ensured everywhere. There has been no vandalism of any kind. Once again the workers have demonstrated their dignity. The maturity of the class destined by history to control the future of their countries has been abundantly proved [*Le Peuple*, 30 June 1968].

Two years later destructive sabotage was still regularly condemned. In January 1970 an accident in the France-Dunkerque yards resulted in the death of a worker; the following month it was 'avenged' by a Maoist group, the 'New People's Resistance': the controls of two cranes were put out of action by short-circuiting the electrical switchboard. The group claimed responsibility. After that there were arson attempts and some small fires were actually lit on ships being built. There was to be an inquiry to decide whether they were accidental or not. However, there was a campaign to blame the Maoists, in which the union federations, especially the C G T, took part, and the earlier sabotage was linked (deliberately or otherwise) with these later provocations. In April 1970 the C G T provincial organization declared its 'strong condemnation of this criminal sabotage ... These fascist-style outrages, which endanger the lives of naval shipyard personnel, have shocked the workers, more especially since they are allowed to go unpunished ... These fascist groups must be disbanded, whatever their supposed allegiance ...' (quoted in Faye, 1973). The unions condemned sabotage – whether genuine or imagined – all the more strongly in that it was likely to distract attention from the real problem: the unsafe working conditions which had caused a number of fatal accidents.

The situation becomes more complex when workers not under any particular leftist influence stop respecting the machinery of production. The strike that occurred during the summer of 1973 at Pechiney-Noguères posed the problem squarely: can production be stopped in continuous-production plants without danger of damage to machinery? Is passive sabotage – by refusing to operate safety services – legitimate? The C G T and the C F D T gave opposite answers to these questions. The C G T did not hold the workers responsible for stopping the electrolysis tanks: they had put no obstacle in the way of managers or foremen who wanted to carry out safety precautions. But fearing that the management might, even so, succeed in making them appear guilty in the eyes of the general public, the C G T called for a return to work. To them it appeared that the only guilty party was the management. And in their statement blaming the management the C G T skilfully exculpated themselves by re-defining their own continuing attitude to the machinery of production as one of 'a spirit of responsibility towards the national interest and towards the future, and taking care to avoid all unilateral action and all provocation' (*La Vie ouvrière*, 1 August 1973). The C F D T made no secret of the dilemma facing its members who worked in continuous-production plants – it openly supported their action and thereby sanctioned their attitude:

If the workers make full use of their right to strike they lay themselves open to the imputation of causing major disruption of the production cycle; but if they let the management dictate the conditions within which they strike (by slowing down production only) then their strike will not achieve its goal, since it will hardly affect the firm financially. The workers wanted to do away with bogus strikes tolerated by management, which left the firm in a position to handle the resulting situation perfectly well [*Syndicalisme-Hebdo*, 3 August 1973].

So the C F D T abandoned the hitherto sacred dogma that the machinery of production must be respected at all costs.

The C F D T also supported the minority strikes in the Lorraine mines early in 1974 – though they were a serious threat to the machinery of production (cf. Barou, 1975). The first was a strike by the railmen who transported coal and coke. Since there were no trucks to move it in, the coke had to stay in the coking furnaces. If the coke goes on burning beyond the eighteen hours necessary to process it, gas escapes, and the ensuing explosion endangers both the coking plant and the gasometer. The leadership had to choose between two courses of action, both of which would result in damage: leaving it to explode, or turning off the heat. By the express wish of the coke workers the railmen agreed to provide a minimum service: they took out the coke in time to remove all risk of explosion, but too late for it to be saleable. The C G T strongly criticized both this first strike, and the second – by 140 quarrymen whose job was to extract sand for filling up the mine galleries. Without it the galleries would collapse, seams would be closed and equipment would be lost under the rubble. This strike was a perfect example of passive sabotage. The C G T attacked the strikers outright: 'The worksites are deteriorating; there are props everywhere to reduce the pressure of earth. It is like a jungle. We order our members to do all they can to fill up the galleries. The situation is extremely serious. The machinery must be saved and safety must be ensured.' The management did not yield to the quarrymen's demands, and they became alarmed and decided to provide 13,000 cubic metres of sand. An engineer's report confirmed that 500m. francs' worth of damage had been done – between lost production, the collapse of one gallery and the destruction of equipment.

The steelworkers' strike at Usinor-Dunkerque in May 1975 posed the same problem as the Pechiney-Noguères strike two years earlier: should safety services be operated in strikes affecting continuous-production industries? In 1975, as in earlier years, an anti-sabotage attitude prevailed at Usinor. Thus the unions could go back to their traditional statements of respect for the machinery of production; then, at dawn on 3 May, the management had the steelworks surrounded by 500 riot police, so as to dislodge the strikers and let in a team of skilled workers to save 8,000 tonnes of metal in the process of being smelted. The CFDT commented: 'The suggestion that there was a danger of solidification was utter bluff. The strikers were supervising the temperature of the smelting process continuously. And in any case the temperature was still far above the danger level of 1,150°. On the contrary, it was the scab workers who damaged the machinery of production; they spoilt nineteen out of twenty-two ladles of steel' (*Synidcalisme-Hebdo*, 15 May 1975). Nor was the C G T's verdict any different: 'The machinery of production was never in any danger. Arrangements had been made to keep the steel at 1,300°. This is proved by the fact that the mixers were emptied without any trouble by the engineers and skilled workers called in by the management' (*La Vie ouvrière*, 14 May 1975).

The CGT theory is straightforward: it respects the machinery of production, and condemns sabotage from whatever quarter; it restrains the enthusiasm of workers who would be prepared to neglect safety precautions by urging them to return to work. The CFDT does not totally support pro-sabotage propaganda; if the workers decide to let other people run some of the machinery slowly so as to avoid the damage that would occur if it stopped completely, then the CFDT will sanction their action. But it will not urge them to do so.

Separate mention must be made of the *Parisien libéré* dispute in 1975 and 1976 which was in the forefront of industrial news for months. Most printing firms are firmly under the control of the CGT Syndicat du Livre. The management of the *Parisien libéré*, faced with the impossibility of getting their paper printed in the usual premises because it was occupied by strikers, decided to get it done in Belgium, or in firms whose workers did not belong to CGT-affiliated unions. This produced a lively reaction from the strikers. On several separate occasions the vans carrying newspapers to retailers were attacked and their contents destroyed, the papers flung down in the road, burnt or otherwise rendered unsaleable. This destruction of the commodity was a clear case of sabotage, and all those involved, either in the theft or the destruction, were in the same CGT union. The CGT did not accept responsibility for the damage, but at no point did it condemn the stand of those who did the burning. The CGT's weekly paper, *La Vie ouvrière*, made no mention of the incidents at all. Did this mean tacit approval – or was it merely that it would have been impossible to express the traditional disapproval without angering the rank and file?

Different forms of strike

In Chapter 1 we considered the forms of strike that cause a real drop in production, i.e., sabotage in our sense: indefinite strikes, strikes with pickets or sit-ins which stop work, 'bottleneck' strikes and go-slows. We must now look at union attitudes to these.

The 'bottleneck' strike – a strike by one workshop or one trade which blocks production from one direction or the other – is recognized by the CFDT. The CGT is more critical:

> The 'bottleneck' strike is nothing new. There have always been partial strikes to block one workshop or one service; they are normally controlled by the unions. When the shutdown of one sector can halt an entire firm we believe that all the workers concerned should be consulted; if they support it, then that kind of strike may lead to a wider dispute. On the other hand, a wildcat stoppage by a small group without consultation with the other workers may well lead to dissensions that the employers can exploit [G. Séguy in *Le Nouvel Observateur*, December, 1969]

Three bottleneck strikes early in 1974 produced a violent debate between the CGT and the CFDT (they were the Lorraine coal strike described above, Moulinex and le Saviem). The CGT recognized that the three disputes made

> justified demands, but they resorted to methods that did more harm than good. The CFDT has produced minority actions if not pure and simple guerrilla tactics ... The CGT does not reject any form of action *a priori*, so it does not condemn the occupation of worksites on principle. But the majority of workers must be in agreement with it. The CFDT believes that a minority can decide. The CGT believes this to be a dangerous proceeding, since such actions result in dissipating the potential of the unions in localized disputes and are no kind of preparation for a large-scale conflict [*La Vie ouvrière*, 27 March 1974].

A year later, when a proliferation of limited strikes gradually paralysed the various Renault establishments, the CGT chose to ignore the fact:

> Do they seriously think anyone believes that this is a case of 'bottleneck' strikes, of unconsidered actions stirred up and led by irresponsible

workers just in order to scuttle the great national company? ... These are not 'bottleneck' strikes. They are not the work of agitators or troublemakers. The work stoppages, most of them lasting only an hour or two, were democratically decided upon by the workers and their CGT and CFDT union militants [*La Vie ouvrière*, 5 March 1975].

This tactic was the same as the one used in the *Parisien libéré* dispute: the CGT could see no value in minority action, but those who put the action into effect considered it very valuable indeed; the CGT therefore chose to ignore it rather than condemn it on principle. To condemn it would have meant a major debate with the CFDT.

The Renault strike in the spring of 1975 also served as an occasion for the unions to adopt a form of action especially effective in lowering production: the go-slow. The workers at Renault Le Mans, who carried out a go-slow for nine weeks, called it a *grève d'enthousiasme* because they worked at times when the management told them not to, and slowed down their work to half-speed when the management authorized normal working. This form of action was illegal: the management un-successfully sued the CGT, demanding damages of six million francs, plus interest, for an estimated loss of 70,000 vehicles. The CFDT approved of this 'original proceeding'; the CGT also supported it since, in this factory where there were 3,000 of its members, it was not a minority action. J. Breteau, the General Secretary of the CGT Metalworkers' Federation, himself declared: 'What the strikers themselves describe as a *grève d'enthousiasme* calls for a strong trade union organization. To do what the workers did at Le Mans, to cut production by half while being at work for the usual time, means subjecting in-dividuals to pressures that can only be countered by rapid and continuous collective resistance' (*La Vie ouvrière*, 23 April 1975). The CGT only accepts majority strikes: that is the decisive criterion as far as it is concerned. This is not the case with the CFDT.

Other forms of sabotage

When they sold the watches at Lip one would have thought that the CGT, with its customary respect for legality, would have condemned this as a clear case of theft. But no. The CGT approved the starting up of the production line, the selling of the watches and the distribution of the money. All this was permissible since it was related to legitimate defence and forced both the management and the government to face up to their responsibilities. It was all the more justified in that the government and the employers had failed to respect legality and that the workers showed a spirit of responsibility where safeguarding machinery was concerned, avoided all divisive, diversionary and provocative tactics, respected the rules of union democracy and enjoyed the sympathy of other workers and the public at large. 'The Lip dispute indicates a heightened class-consciousness in the workers. In this sense, yes, we repeat: the Lip workers' action is a valuable experiment from which we can all learn something' (G. Séguy in, *Le Nouvel Observateur*, 6 September 1973).

The CFDT also saw the action at Lip as a form of self-defence. Their illegal action became legitimate because it altered the balance of forces in their favour: the fighting spirit of the workers was strengthened, public sympathy was won over and a wave of solidarity was created. The initiative was with the workers the whole time, the money from the sale of the watches ensured their survival and everything that was done was decided collectively and done by all. But, unlike the CGT, the CFDT also saw the Lip workers' action as making a breach in capitalist law (the law of property, the law that work-contracts can be unilaterally broken) which the ruling class identified as the law of justice, the one and only law conceivable. It further provided a glimpse of the possibility of a different sort of society, proving that the managers were not indispensable, that the workers could organize and run their own work, that a new type of less hierarchical work relationships could exist. In similar disputes which followed the Lip conflict the CFDT continued to support workers who sold goods they had collectively expropriated.

The unions have had little to say about more individual forms of sabotage, such as the flight from industrial jobs, labour turnover and absenteeism. However, in 1970–71, during the negotiations over monthly salary status that were to result in larger payments for justified absence from work, they found an occasion to express their attitude to absenteeism. They strongly objected to the clauses that made the continuance of sick pay after a trial period depend on there being no rise in the rate of absenteeism; they further opposed any medical checks by management. If this meant that they connived at workers' taking advantage of the system to stay away without justification, then clearly they were accepting this form of sabotage. But perhaps it merely meant that they linked a possible increase in the rate of absenteeism with a foreseeable deterioration in working conditions in the future, or indeed with the possibility that workers might now be able to take better care of their health? It seems to have been this last consideration that motivated them during the negotiations – but in ensuring the conditions they wanted they were inevitably also supporting absenteeism as a form of sabotage.

An overall view

The CGT disapproves all instances of sabotage to destroy machinery, and stipulates certain conditions for such forms of strike as 'bottleneck' strikes and go-slows; however, it approved the action of the Lip workers. The CFDT is readier to legitimate all such illegal actions. What makes an action legitimate? Why have the unions in recent years produced texts discussing methods of action which leave their theories so vague and undefined? Very often the attitudes they adopt while some action is actually taking place are much clearer.

At the CGT congress at Le Bourget in June 1975 G. Séguy touched on the problem of different forms of action. He said:

> The savage resistance to workers' demands by employers and the State-as-employer inspires our confederation to seek the most effective possible forms of struggle and those best adapted to situations as they

arise, to do everything to avoid having our backs to the wall. It is natural for workers to act in ways that will not cost them too much. Nevertheless it remains indispensable to plan our struggles in a responsible way ... In other words, there must be a systematic exercise of union democracy which enables all our members to share in the working out of decisions, thus extending workers' democracy to the level of all wage-earners.

The CGT again stresses the role of the union organization as prime mover (not caring to find itself faced with a *fait accompli*) and advocates cohesive mass actions that will get all needful support from the public.

The CFDT has its criteria for legitimate action too:

It is up to the unions to keep the workers generally informed, to bring them together for collective discussion, to suggest analyses, objectives, forms of struggle suited to the circumstances, to create the conditions for genuine participation by all the workers in a dispute in determining their action ... This line of thought is not compatible with the notion of an enlightened vanguard that claims to lead the workers' struggle, or the manipulative practices of minorities [*Syndicalisme-Hebdo*, 28 March 1974].

Officially, then, there is little difference between this and the CGT position. But in practice the CFDT is more readily swept along by movements rising from the grassroots, however illegal they may be.

Despite their differences, the CGT and the CFDT signed the agreement of June 1974 which, for the first time in trade union history, included a joint statement on methods of action. The statement is a compromise. It passes judgement on no specific form of action. It emphasizes the 'responsibility of the trade union organizations', 'the ever more active and widespread participation of the workers in democractic discussion and in all decisions regarding the implementation of actions'. Forms of action must 'allow for the risks of isolation and division', 'have the support of other wage-earners and the general public'. In other words, both organizations reserved the right to judge every case on its own merits. The text is vague enough to make it clear that their views about forms of action by no means coincide: it neither approves nor condemns any specific practices. However, destructive sabotage is implicitly condemned, since it seems unlikely to get support from most of the general public.

CGT theory regarding forms of action is consistent: its strategy makes it self-explanatory. The crisis of capitalism means that workers must strive both for immediate day-to-day gains and for those deeper transformations of society that can be attained only after a broad alliance of anti-monopolist forces has won electoral victory. The second aim seems to us the more important. The CGT has absorbed the lessons of 1968, with the failure of the left in the June elections. Any form of action that fails to get popular support and/or accentuates the divisions among the working class, and thus impedes electoral strategy, is to be deprecated. On the other hand the CGT may be led to support really tough action as long as it involves a large majority of workers, does not widen the gulf between workers and trade union activists and is popular with public opinion – at least providing no election is in the immediate offing. Apart from its condemnation of damage to machines which is unvarying, the CGT will judge each case as it arises: Will this action mean a loss of votes for the left, or not? It condemns the sabotaging of machines for that reason, but also for another: it wants to see a socialist society, based on the steady development of production – and since such development is only rendered possible by machinery, no machinery must be sabotaged, either now or in the socialist future.

CFDT theory is also linked with its strategy for achieving socialism – but it is a much less election-oriented strategy than the CGT's. In its 1974 statement on the Union of the Left we read:

The CFDT wants to develop mass and class action which will make social struggles the moving force for transforming society ... The conquest of political power does not consist only in achieving a left-wing electoral majority; the occasion might well not be an election, but a social crisis. The phase of transition to socialism cannot begin without full mastery of political power, which involves the conquest of the prevailing economic and cultural order as well as control of the apparatus of government. Consequently, there must be such a strong and purposeful mobilization that the left, once it achieves a majority, can effect significant changes directed both to mastering and transforming political power and to starting to build up socialism based on workers' self-management. Power will thus be won by a combination of convergent and complementary social and political struggles.

The weight the CFDT attaches to social struggles explains the high value set on workers' combativity – even when exercised outside the framework of legality. What matters is not the form of struggle, but the struggle itself, the workers' demonstration of their opposition to the employers as well as of their capacity to manage their own affairs. Once one realizes this, it is easier to understand the CFDT's support for the workers at Pechiney or the Lorraine collieries. A strike can impede the strategy of the CGT; but, in theory, the only strike that could damage CFDT strategy would be one that aimed at destroying trade union organization.

The situation in Britain

In Great Britain, as we have seen, violence and sabotage were often associated with early trade unionism, a kind of 'collective bargaining by riot'. As the trade unions grew stronger, however, they condemned these acts. Robert Applegarth, the General Secretary of the Amalgamated Society of Carpenters and Joiners and the leading trade unionist of his time, was at great pains to persuade his members 'that the most effective form of collective bargaining was not always the most noisy and seldom the most violent' (Briggs, 1965).

In 1866, following a series of notorious disturbances in Sheffield which become known as the 'Sheffield outrages', the government appointed a Royal Commission on Trade Unions to look into the whole position of trade unions in society. At this period Applegarth and his fellow trade union leaders were endeavouring to present unionism in a favourable light. In his evidence to the Commission, at which he was the most important union witness, Applegarth consolidated this policy of respectability. 'He held up the ideal of cooperation between masters and men and supported the beginnings of a system of voluntary understanding, which eventually was to become the guiding principle of British industrial relations' (Briggs, 1965). The conventionality shown by Applegarth and his fellow union leaders at this crucial time proved to be a characteristic of later trade unionism, particularly of the leaders.

Today it is common for the unions, and especially shop stewards, to support forms of action resulting in a loss of production, but not necessarily in damage to machinery or goods. Furthermore, restrictive practices are often formalized in collective agreements (in other words, the unions have sought to legitimize behaviour by workers that would prevent increases in productivity).

Strikes are not the only means used by the unions in Britain in pursuit of their members' demands. In the last century craftsmen used to formulate their own working rules, and the employers had to accept them; they refused to work in any establishment that did not abide by them. This was in fact a form of action that stopped production completely for recalcitrant employers. Shop stewards today have no hesitation in condoning other kinds of disruption (McCarthy, 1969). First of all, they may refuse to cooperate: when working relations in a plant are good they may assist the management by urging workers not to stay away, to work slowly, or knock off work early, and by persuading them to agree to changes in working teams or positions on the assembly-line. If relations deteriorate, however, they may withdraw such help. Secondly, they may insist to a greater or lesser extent on certain formal rights and customs: to hold up production while a dispute is going on, they can reintroduce regulations that have fallen into disuse but were never formally repealed (in Britain, verbal agreements still have considerable importance). Going slow – more or less organized, more or less widespread – is one form of action that is used a lot in industry, either directly to stabilize wages or to ensure that there will be overtime (if the work does not get done in the expected time the employer will have to pay for overtime), or simply as one element in the total context of negotiations. Finally, there is action to shorten working hours – refusing to work through Saturday night, for instance, or to cover for workers who are ill. In Britain actions like these are implicitly approved by the unions, and shop stewards will quite often be the instigators of them.

Loss of production may result not only from the occasional recourse to special forms of action, but also from regular practices actually written into collective agreements. It was against such restrictive practices that the various productivity agreements of the sixties were framed. Historically, they follow from the fact that British trade unionism was for so long based on craft unions. What form do they take? First, there is the regular dependence on overtime working; this demonstrates, on the one hand, the fact that a great many managements are incapable of estimating how long a particular job should take and, on the other, the power of the unions in managing to control the number of hours worked. Then there is the rigid demarcation of jobs as between different groups of workers; this enables skilled workers to retain their power and their value, and gives them a strong bargaining position; its most important effect is to limit access to certain jobs by demanding lengthy apprenticeships. Then, too, there is the speed limit imposed on transport vehicles: for a long time now the TGWU has tried to restrict the speed of industrial vehicles to well below the legal speed limit; reasons of safety have always been adduced for this calculated slowing down. Despite all the efforts made in the middle sixties to cut down such restrictive practices, they still proliferate in British industry, and they have full support from the unions on the shop floor (Clegg, 1972).

Maoists and sabotage

I want to end this chapter with an analysis of the doctrines of the present-day far left, in particular the Maoists. It has no influence on trade union theory, but is worth our study because these are the few political groups that approve of actively destructive sabotage (not merely such passive action as refusing to operate safety services).

Back in 1965 the Maoist paper *L'Humanité nouvelle* (4 May) urged its readers to take tougher forms of action:

To the dictatorship of the exploiting classes we must oppose a dictatorship of the exploited class. We must fight this difficult class struggle with unwavering determination, and be prepared with our eyes open for every form of struggle the situation may impose, without exception [quoted in Kessel, 1972].

A year later the paper openly advocated threats of sabotage (18 May 1966):

To a company, the real threat is the danger of damage to its industrial installations, not just the possibility of a production stoppage. Their plant is worth millions. Though it costs them a lot when production stops, there can be no comparison between the two. Only the fear of having to invest huge new amounts of capital will defeat them, for a monopoly can always tolerate the prospect of losses, even quite large ones.

Workers must use the threat of sabotage by occupying their workplaces during strikes; sabotage by neglecting safety precautions will be put into effect if the police intervene:

The employers will be forced to negotiate when workers occupy the premises, because their costly installations will be our hostage in case of violence by the state police [*L'Humanité nouvelle*, 17 April 1967].

This sentence was written at a time when factory occupations had virtually ceased to happen. They reappeared in the strikes of 1968, but sabotage was not used to counter police intervention. So the Maoist group's diagnosis would seem to have been mistaken.

After 1968 some Maoist groups spoke in support of sabotage when it occurred. In August 1971, when workers from the Brandt works in Lyon were imprisoned for sabotage, the Maoists defended them. Under the heading 'Sabotage should not be a traceable action,' the paper *J'accuse* (1 November 1971) described successful sabotage:

The boss always wants to make an example – to strike down a few strong-minded people so as to intimidate everyone else. That is why the Brandt workers think sabotage should be much more carefully planned. Not merely technically planned, to ensure that the author cannot be spotted, but planned ahead by identifying anyone who might be an informer. And even more by preparing one's fellow-workers: they must understand the reason for the sabotage. They must want to do the same thing, and be able to do it when their turn comes.

A leaflet handed round at Peugeot also recommended sabotage:

We must take the offensive *now:* think up forms of sabotage, ways of slowing down production; take longer tea-breaks, cut wires, forget to put in bolts, lose tools. What finishes the bosses is when we discover that it is only our sweat that keeps them going. Well, we are our own masters now; we must seize the initiative from those who shackle or deflect strike action – starting with the unions [quoted in Dumont, 1972].

These extracts show some of what Maoists see as the aims of sabotage – making struggles over demands effective, vengeance, workers' control of production. In his book, *Les Maoïstes français*, Rémi Hess stresses this last tendency:

Inserting an iron bar into the line may be reminiscent of Luddism, but it is in fact preparation for massive action against the whole system of assembly-line work ... The Maoists propose workers' control in place of the organization of work which the employers have set up in the firm. As against the bourgeoisie's work organization on a basis of meaningless hierarchies, they propose a workers' organization that offers an all-embracing political and social alternative.

But it was undoubtedly the group who, in 1974, published *De la grève sauvage à l'autogestion généralisée*, under the pseudonym Ratgeb, who gave the widest significance to sabotage. It must aim not only to demystify labour as a value in itself, to conserve workers' energies or to take revenge. It must also be directed towards revolution. The group's A B C of revolution was as follows:

A. The aim of sabotage or expropriation, whether individual or collective, is to launch a wildcat strike. B. Every unofficial strike should turn into an occupation. C. Every occupied factory should be taken over and used directly to assist the revolutionaries. D. In electing delegates (whose job is to record their decisions and get them carried out, and who can be dismissed at any time) the strikers' assembly is laying the bases of a radically new organization: totally self-managed industry.

This revolutionary strategy, which passes so rapidly from sabotage to self-management, may raise a smile – indeed, the whole book seems more like a hoax than anything else.

Summary

Organized or unorganized groups in industry declare themselves for or against different forms of sabotage depending on what political or pragmatic aims they see as most important. There are two opposing schools of thought: the Marxist school, which is against sabotage, since it is an obstacle to the total transformation of society and the unimpeded growth of production; and the anarchist school, which has no hesitation in advocating sabotage if it will lead to an immediate improvement in working conditions.

The question is whether either of them has much influence on what actually happens. Concrete events certainly help to determine the theories; does it work both ways? Early in this century the CGT was in favour of sabotage, but there was very little sabotage in the workplace. Today some forms of sabotage are spreading, yet the prevailing theory, that of the CGT, is hostile to the practice. Furthermore, though the CFDT is prepared to legitimate some instances of sabotage *after* they have occurred, it certainly does not offer any sort of apologia for the practice. Finally, those groups that have declared themselves in favour have virtually no audience among industrial workers. Thus it appears that sabotage runs counter to the official theory of the organized groups to which by far the majority of workers belong. Who then are the saboteurs?

4 The Saboteurs

If the union federations to which the vast majority of the French working class belong, the CGT and the CFDT, almost always condemn the destructive sabotaging of machinery and goods, sometimes hesitate to support last-ditch strikes and make no mention at all in their statements of such forms of action as absenteeism, then, logically, the saboteurs cannot be in the mainstream of the trade union movement. Who are they?

One school of commentators concludes that saboteurs come from among non-unionized workers – the unskilled, those employed in new industries or newly industrialized layers of the working class, the young and/or inexperienced, people employed in small firms. Some of the evidence would support this theory, but there is quite a lot of contrary evidence as well.

A second school maintains that sabotage can be the work of skilled workers, or workers politically organized outside their unions. In condemning sabotage, the national organizations simply do not represent the attitudes of their rank and file. Some would say that the summit knows very well what is going on at the base, and lets it happen, while making a parade of hostility. I myself also believe that the spread of sabotage indicates a determination by the rank and file to make their own decisions. The waves of strikes in the late 1960s resulted in giving the rank and file far more power.

A third school of commentators, ignoring the question of union membership, thinks that what matters is the position the saboteurs hold in the production process: those workers, whether skilled or not, who hold a key position from which they could instantly paralyse the whole process, are the ones likely to become saboteurs. These workers become organized on the basis of a kind of technical corporatism. This explanation cannot possibly cover all forms of sabotage: however, the technicalities of work certainly have some influence on the type of sabotage to which workers resort.

I believe, myself, that all these factors are significant. However, I also think that any instance of sabotage can be understood better if it is seen in the context of the history of the firm concerned. There are periods of sabotage, just as there are periods of strictly legal action. Every firm reproduces these phases on its own time-scale, depending on such factors as how long it has been in existence. This difference explains some of the apparent contradictions that cannot be accounted for in the foregoing analyses, since they are necessarily too static.

Sabotage by marginal groups

The theory of sabotage by unskilled workers can be summed up as follows:

The French trade union movement has never embraced more than a part of the working class – skilled workers, workers in specialized trades, people with a relatively long industrial tradition. Those who are outside the control of the unions choose their forms of action without reference to the attitudes adopted by the national organizations. During any period when industry is absorbing larger numbers of workers, there is always an increase in acts of sabotage.

But who are they, this massive marginal working class? Some would reply that they are a class brought into factory jobs by the changing pattern of industry – former farmworkers and artisans whose skills are irrelevant to their new jobs: these are supposedly the saboteurs we are looking for. The great strike of 1877 in the United States, a kind of general strike that started in the railways and then spread to other industries, saw a proliferation of different forms of sabotage (in Pittsburgh 104 locomotives, over 2,000 carriages and the station buildings were destroyed). It was caused by the meteoric industrialization that took place following the Civil War, when thousands of people from farms and small workshops found themselves in factories.

There was no organization they could join, and the first period of economic depression caused an eruption of violence. It was a spontaneous and violent movement, typical of new industrialization (Brecher, 1972).

The wave of violent strikes in France in the 1880s and 1890s was related to the existence of unstructured workers' organizations following rapid socio-economic change (Shorter and Tilly, 1971). The migration of country people to the towns, and of handcraft workers into industry, produced a new industrial workforce in a state of social disorganization. The workers lost the moral beliefs they had had before, and felt a surge of hatred against those responsible for their present discomforts. M. Perrot also says of the strikes of that period: 'In those pre-trade-union days, strikes were not so much a result of planning as of emotion or anger. People crowded together and made threatening gestures; there was frequently violence, and sometimes little else.' Violence was commoner in the straggling villages that were 'the first stages of rural emigration, of the formation of the working class'.

Industrialization goes through successive phases. A number of European countries became heavily industrialized in the years between 1960 and 1970, France especially. The proportion of employed wage-earners increased by 23·08 per cent from 1962 to 1973: there was a 14·4 per cent increase in industry and building, 49·5 per cent in transport, services and trade, 45·6 per cent in administrative work; the change took place in two main periods, the early 1960s and 1969–73. In Belgium the increase was 15·85 per cent, in Italy 5·68 per cent and in Germany 4·3 per cent. The new workers were taken on either in existing factories which expanded to accommodate them, or in new factories in areas where there had been little industry before, or in new sectors of activity (services and trade). The question is whether this mass of new workers has played a part in the present-day spread of sabotage. In the view of S. Mallet, those who have recently been absorbed into the exploited working population resort to tough and illegal forms of action similar to those used by the workers who became industrialized at the end of the last century. Such unskilled workers tend to be employed in factories away from the cities, cut off both from other factories and from their own research and technology departments. Types of struggle spread by contagion, by a 'continuous chain of movements each affecting the next'. A new plant like General Motors at Lordstown was subject to a great deal of sabotage in the early 1970s.

Newly industrialized workers commit sabotage. They hold the least skilled jobs in industry, and the unskilled commit sabotage. Who are the individuals who go to make up this new proletariat? Former farmworkers and artisans, of course, but also, by extension, all those who have been employed for a shorter than average time: young people, women, immigrants. Young people are prone to certain sorts of sabotage (Rousselet, 1974): refusing to work in industry and preferring to set up in a small way on their own, avoidance of employment, not looking for a job when they first leave school, frequent job-changes, working apathetically or even with positive distaste for what they are doing, leaving apprenticeships without good reason. Women are prone to other forms of sabotage: their absenteeism, which is markedly higher than that of men, is the bane of all industries; nor is it merely connected with having children. Mallet notes the high incidence of strikes among unskilled women in the clothing and electrical-goods trades.

According to the theory that workers without any long industrial tradition tend to commit sabotage, we should also expect to find that immigrants do so. In recent years immigrants have certainly been responsible for some very long strikes, but on the whole they have not been violent ones. In our study of the strikes of 1971 we concluded that there was no more illegal action in firms employing large numbers of women, young people and immigrants – i.e., a workforce with generally little industrial tradition – than anywhere else (Dubois and Durand, 1975).

There is, then, no positive confirmation of the theory that sabotage can be linked with absence of industrial tradition or skill on the part of workers. Indeed, there is some concrete evidence against it. That unskilled workers will commit sabotage where the skilled would not is untrue. In strikes where the majority of workers involved are skilled, there are just as many tough actions as where all the strikers are unskilled. At Lip, for instance, the proposal to slow down the rate of production, which was chosen as the first form of action, came from the engineering workers, not those on the assembly-line. At the beginning this action was not popular with them at all: 'We'd rather strike for two hours a day; it would have the same effect and we'd know exactly what we're doing. Working slowly like this is really hard: we've got the foreman breathing down our necks, and management coming down on us, and we're not really equipped to stand up to them' (quoted in Piaget, 1973). In fact, to make the slowing-down effective the Lip workers had to put an engineer beside the assembly-line all day, to explain just what must be done to reduce production. In the last century, too, the workers who broke machines were the most highly skilled, who saw the machines as a threat to their status.

Nor is it true that young people commit sabotage whereas older people do not. In their analysis of a recurrent series of go-slows in one Hungarian firm, Hethy and Mako (1971) showed that it was the older workers who were responsible. When management lowered piece-rates, the older workers worked more slowly in order to make them return to a reasonable payment. They could sustain the resulting drop in earnings because they could no longer expect any increase in wages (there were no pay rises for anyone over the age of thirty), because they had no debts and were therefore more independent, and because their length of employment and relatively high level of skill combined to foster a strong, informal group structure which gave them support. The young workers, on the other hand, did not go slow: they produced more than usual, because they wanted to make up for the loss of earnings decreed by management. They acted for precisely the opposite reasons from those which led the older workers to go slow.

P. Bernoux also undermines the hypothesis of a correlation between absence of industrial tradition and sabotage. In the firm where he worked, he found that it was not the newer workers (peasant workers and immigrants) who cut down production, but those who came from an industrial working-class background. Workers from the country produced as much as usual, or even more. They felt no involvement in the firm, because their real interest lay with their smallholdings in the country; they still shared in the collective mentality of their culture of origin – submission, respect for their superiors, fatalism, a sense that it was safest to do what one was told in this alien world. Immigrants varied: those hoping to return to their homes were model workers; those planning to have a career in industry in France had no hesitation in slowing down production rates. So career plans modify attitudes to work and the likelihood of resorting to sabotage; those intending to stay in industry, especially where there was no option, were prepared to express opposition by operating a go-slow; they were committed to a long-term struggle.

Finally, are workers who are only recently signed on more likely to be saboteurs? No. The workers who went on strike at the Lorraine collieries early in 1974 and disregarded all safety regulations (see Chapter 3, p. 112, above) were not newcomers to industrial work. They were former miners unable to go down the pits any longer, who in changing jobs had lost status. They were not men without industrial traditions, but embittered men.

If the theory that it is lack of industrial experience – whether among the formerly self-employed, immigrants, young people, women, or workers only recently signed on – is not adequate to explain how acts of sabotage come about, we must consider other explanations.

Sabotage by some union workers

Despite official theories to the contrary, sabotage *is* sometimes associated with workers who belong – or who once belonged – to unions. This may be because the leadership has not yet gained control over its rank and file, or because it leaves them free to make their own decisions, or because it has lost the control it once had.

When a union has only recently become established in a firm it is often faced with a large new group that it is hard for the central union organization to control. The workers, as yet unversed in the theory of the organization they have just joined, have no hesitation in resorting to certain forms of sabotage, such as indefinite strikes, stopping the movement of goods and refusing to operate safety services. In one French sweet factory there was a strike that lasted for fourteen weeks just after the plant had become unionized; the strikers set up pickets to prevent all merchandise from entering the premises and all goods produced from leaving (Karsh, 1958). In our study of strikes in 1971 we found the same thing: illegal strikes happened most often where the tradition of striking was of recent date or where the union had not been long established (Dubois and Durand, 1975).

The union may leave its rank and file free to choose their own forms of action. This could be a stratagem. There can be a complex interplay between the reformist leader who does the negotiating and the workers who carry out violent actions on the shop floor. The leader urges the employers to satisfy the justified grievances of his members – otherwise he cannot be responsible for controlling them. It might suit him quite well if a gang of disorderly youths should happen to fulfil his prophecies at that very moment (Nieburg, 1963). Some unions opt for a policy of decentralization in decision-making, in keeping with their general attitude – for example, the C F D T. It is not surprising that where the C F D T members are in the majority – or even in significant numbers – tougher and less legal forms of action tend to occur. The rank and file are more likely to make their own decisions independent of the union federations if they have a choice between competing organizations: one of the federations will always be tempted to outbid the other by supporting sabotage if that seems likely to bring it some advantage.

Sabotage will also be used in places where the union organization controls negotiations and official demands, but not the forms of action used on the shop floor to win immediate concessions. Situations of this sort may be classified as sabotage outside the trade union movement. In British firms most of the action taken to limit managerial authority (go-slows, restricting production) does not come from official trade union institutions but is spontaneously organized by workers at shop-floor level (Hyman, 1972). The same is true of the United States:

The strikers of the 1930s, when they were taking part in direct actions or occupations, believed that the solution to their problems lay in the setting up of trade unions, government departments and Welfare offices. Today, sabotage is a final answer to the obsolescence of that form of social organization; people no longer want to create structures, but rather to use direct action to get immediate solutions to problems; this still calls for solidarity and organization, but it does not require representation by a specialized leadership like the trade union [Brecher, 1972].

The union is there but the members act independently of it. This situation exists in eastern-bloc countries also: the go-slow referred to earlier in a Hungarian firm was managed by an unofficial workers' organization based on shared length of employment or shared skills. The official union did not approve their action, and in fact actually supported the management decision to cut wages which was the immediate cause of the go-slow (Hethy and Mako, 1971). In French firms the chances of sabotage are greatest where there are political groups alongside the unions: the presence of members of the P S U* or far-left organizations usually means an increase in illegality, whereas when the C P is the only organized group there is less likely to be tough action (Dubois and Durand, 1975).

The offensive by the rank and file

Finally, and above all, the spread of various forms of sabotage in the past few years is due to workers on the shop floor having a greater say over what forms of struggle they will adopt. The fact that some unions now leave their membership free in this respect is directly due to shop-floor pressure. People can decide on the most appropriate form of action in relation to their own particular situation, and may well decide on sabotage if it seems advantageous. They do not have to keep the national political situation constantly in view. It is largely this increasing role played by workers as a whole in running their own struggles that explains the increase in sabotage. How can this be seen in western Europe?

*Parti Socialiste Unifié: a left split from the Socialist Party.

In France before 1968 there was little control over forms of action by the rank and file; the right of workers to meet in the workplace, which they were beginning to demand, was not yet recognized, nor was there any official right to organize a trade union in one's place of work; any action was started and kept under control by union militants. During May and June 1968 there was a radical change in the mobilization of workers, with the rise of new bodies for running strikes – workers' assemblies and strike committees. At the time the strikes began, control by workers' assemblies was not significant (though some people thought it was), but it became decisive as the struggle went on; however, it was thwarted by pressure from the central federations to return to work as the elections drew near. But the control the ordinary workers won at that time was not just a flash in the pan. Thenceforth there was incessant debate in the union federations on the subject of democracy during disputes: on the opposition or complementarity of union democracy (with decisions made by union members) and workers' democracy (with decisions made by the whole of the workforce concerned); on methods of voting; on the role of the union in the workers' assemblies; on strike committees. Though it showed how far they still had to go, that debate demonstrated the increasing power of the rank and file. So did the spread of strikes in individual firms; and workers' assemblies on the shop floor became more and more frequent, despite the fact that they were not officially recognized.

In Italy the same process occurred, and it too led to much greater control by the rank and file. But, unlike France, the structures set up during the high point of the struggle in 1968–9 (assemblies and delegates) were subsequently formalized. Before the events of autumn 1969 the situation was that the trade union leadership decided upon an action, and its local section decided to put it into effect in this or that firm. The bodies representing the workers in those firms (the works committee and union section) had no share at all in decisions about disputes. They were not even asked to give an opinion. From the summer of 1968 to the autumn of 1969 the situation gradually changed. The committees of workers and students which were set up around certain firms advocated the management of disputes by the workers themselves, direct democracy in the workers' assembly (with choice of the forms of confrontation and the kinds of demand to be made), and direct action (the workers themselves to control their pace of work). Elsewhere, spontaneous strikes occurred, without official authorization, and with no official union control over their development. It was during the course of such strikes that workers appointed the first delegates and strike committees – independent of the works committee – whom they could themselves dismiss and whom they could really supervise because they were elected from among a homogeneous group. Their function was to express and negotiate the group's demands and boost its struggle. These delegates supported the acts of sabotage carried out by the workers, at Fiat for instance. In the years that followed the situation changed yet again. From the spring of 1969 onwards the unions supported the holding of referendums in the firms concerned to determine the form of any dispute. These new structures for organizing disputes were then formalized: there were a number of agreements which recognized delegates and factory councils, and the right of assembly was enshrined in official labour legislation in May 1970. From 1970, then, a new phase opened in the whole system of dispute regulation, with a complicated interaction between the leadership and the rank and file. If we examine the way the problem of controlling disputes developed in Italy, we find, as in France, a much larger part being played by the rank and file – with spontaneous strikes, the election of strike delegates and the holding of workers' assemblies in the workplace. This process of decentralization, alternately supported and restrained by the union federations, explains the spread of sabotage directed to improving working conditions (slowing down work-rates, bottlenecks in the production line, etc.)

In Germany we also find the role of the rank and file growing after 1968, but less markedly than in France and Italy. There was a considerable rise in spontaneous strikes, which disrupted production processes and were in that sense sabotage. In Germany an official strike, which can only be called by the union after collective bargaining has failed and 75 per cent of union members have approved the decision to strike, takes lengthy preparation. There can be absolutely no hope of using surprise tactics. When we add to this the fact that a strike can be stopped at any time by 25 per cent of those involved in it, it becomes clear how little disruption can be caused by that means. However, under pressure from the rank and file such official strikes became longer and more numerous, and thus led to a drop in production. The importance of the rank and file which this demonstrated became more marked with the upsurge of spontaneous strikes (starting in 1966–7, but reaching a peak in 1969) – strikes not called by the unions and not following regulation procedure, which broke agreements still in force and had a strong surprise element. The unions found themselves being forced into starting official strikes to give expression to the combative spirit of their membership. This growing control by the rank and file was also noteworthy for the larger part now played by union delegates on the shop floor in instigating spontaneous strikes.

In Great Britain the rank and file have always had a lot of control; what is new in recent years has been that the authorities have tried in vain to counter it by introducing more rigorous strike legislation. It is traditional in Britain to distinguish three ways in which a strike may start: wildcat strikes are those which disregard conventional procedures and are not recognized by any of the representative structures of the workforce. Unofficial strikes, on the other hand, are supported by the shop stewards in the firm concerned but not by the union outside it. An official strike can only be called by the union as such. A strike often changes from one type to another: a spontaneous strike may be made official. But when the union has decided on a return to work, if the strikers are not satisfied with the agreements reached unofficial actions may start up again. An unofficial strike is completely under the control of the workers – at the beginning, during its progress and in its ending. It is not a new phenomenon, but it is the most frequent type of strike. What is new, in recent years, is that both Conservative and Labour governments have done their best to combat this powerful control by the workers. Labour failed with Barbara Castle's *In Place of Strife;* the Conservatives succeeded for a time with Robert Carr's Industrial Relations Act in 1971 (which made the unions responsible for all unofficial strikes: the Industrial Relations Court could fine them and demand compensation); but in the event this law aroused such hostility among workers that it became a dead letter even before the Conservatives fell from office in 1974. The extent of shop-floor control in England explains the spread of restrictive practices (increasingly embodied in collective agreements), a real form of sabotage (see Chapter 2 above).

In Belgium the amount of control the workers have is clear from the frequency of spontaneous strikes – against the advice of the unions and without their approval. The position was to some extent formalized by the economic and social conference held in 1970 following a wave of such strikes: since then workers have had the right to hold meetings at their workplace and during working hours.

Thus growing control by workers in general over their own struggles is manifested in different ways in different countries: there are spontaneous strikes, and new structures are set up as a result (workers' assemblies, strike committees, new methods of voting). Not only is there a tendency for strikes to be called more often within the individual firm, but there is also an increase in a number of different forms of action, which may well include sabotage. In the period 1968–70 this control by workers on the shop floor got somewhat out of hand, but it became routinized afterwards: in some cases it was formalized by law (the right of assembly at the workplace was made official, for instance); the unions reinforced the role of their organizational structure at shop-floor level with an obvious hope both of trying to be more representative of their grass roots and of keeping the initiative in future. With increasing formalization, the spread of sabotage could once again be held in check by pressure from the trade union organizations opposed to it.

Technical and organizational rationalization

The control which industrial workers have come to exercise over their own disputes, leading to the spread of tougher forms of action such as sabotage, has been a victory: it was won by the great waves of strikes in the period 1968–70. Sometimes it depended on a technical rationalization of production, which gave particular groups of workers a greater opportunity for disruption.

'The extension of technology has brought an enormous imbalance between the possibilities of attack and the means of defence. It facilitates or allows of a geometrical progression in the amount of damage that can be done and a fantastic disproportion between the slight risk incurred by the perpetrator and the cost of the damage he or she can inflict' (Sartori, 1972).

Production processes are becoming more and more fully integrated, which leads to more attempts to obstruct them. Radical action by workers traditionally appeared in settings characterized by two phenomena: the arrival on the scene of large numbers of people hitherto without voice or influence (we noted above the links between sabotage and the absence of industrial tradition) and subsistence-level existence among the working class. Today radicalism is returning with technological development, but the context is now different: there is powerful political representation for workers, and the economy is one of relative abundance.

Two instances will illustrate the importance of complex technology and the power it puts in the hands of certain groups of workers in modern industry in terms of sabotage. In one steelworks the computer technicians began an indefinite strike for higher wages; this disrupted the working of the plant and the payment of all wages. Management fought back by trying to send tapes out to be processed elsewhere, but the technicians responded by stealing one of the tapes. Another case was the threat of a selective strike by nuclear power station process workers: not merely was their work indispensable to production, but if they struck completely there would be immediate damage to the installations – and, even worse, the risk of radioactive contamination of the atmosphere (Barrier, 1975). Bottleneck strikes also illustrate the importance of the technological context.

Technological development makes industry more vulnerable to sabotage, but similarly the development of industrial organization also has major consequences. The mounting complexity of the commodities produced, the increasing division of labour, the reduction of stocks, the ever-greater importance of fixed capital, the numbers of managerial and office staff who still have to be paid when the workers are on indefinite strike, the small margin of cash funds – all these features of modern industry mean that even the smallest disruption can be more disastrous than ever before.

But not all sabotage occurs in the firms with the most advanced technical and organizational development. Some types, such as the go-slow, are typical of more traditional forms of work organization. Others are to be found in all types of industry – the sabotaging of machines, arson, indefinite strikes, absenteeism, labour turnover. In small industries, or in the non-mechanized sections of large firms – in other words where the worker really makes what he produces without having to fit into a constricting system of work organization – it is easy to sabotage what you are producing. Action by this type of skilled worker may become less effective when the work system starts to be rationalized with a view to mass production, so any change in system is likely to be a threat. With the *Parisien libéré*, the reduction in numbers printed and subsequent destruction of those printed abroad to prevent their distribution in France, were typical of a concern where the workers are powerful both because of their skill and experience and because of the cohesiveness of their union: that power they can turn against certain modernizing measures. Even in mass-production industries the unskilled worker still has physical contact with what he is producing; at a prescribed pace, and within strict limitations, he acts on it to transform it; therefore sabotage, either direct or by going slow, is still possible. But, in highly automated industry, where the worker traces the progress of the product via a series of signals, the only way he can sabotage the product is by interfering with the machinery. There is no scope for going slow, then, but there is scope for sabotaging the machinery; this is also the ideal situation for bottleneck strikes and refusing to operate safety services.

Slowing down production is a form of sabotage which largely depends on the way work is organized. Its greatest possibilities for disruption are when there is very little supervision of work by departments outside the workshop itself, when the job each worker must do is not very precisely demarcated, when production is not highly integrated (whether in terms of production processes or of individual workers) and when the worker has power to determine the quantity of production. Going slow is therefore a form of action that we find in craft industries and mass-production industries.

The incidence of theft is not haphazard, either. Theft of tools can only happen in industries where the workers use easily portable tools. Theft of products only occurs in assembly-line industries which produce consumer goods small enough to be carried away unnoticed.

Thus the technological and organizational development of industry increases the likelihood of new types of sabotage emerging, based on the paralysing disruption created by the stoppage of specific key points of production. However, though there now exist highly automated industries, that does not mean that all craft industries and, still more, all assembly-line industries have disappeared. Even in a single firm, different work sectors can operate at different levels of development. So, the variety of technical levels allows of a variety of forms of sabotage.

Sabotage and the history of past disputes

The spread of sabotage in the present day can be explained, then, for various reasons, by all these factors we have spoken of: the entry of new groups of workers into industry and services and the fact that they are not unionized, the increased control of their own disputes that workers as a whole have gained, and the technological development that has produced the new highly automated industrial complexes.

However, we do not find sabotage occurring at the same moment in every firm: there is, in each case, a history of sabotage that can in part be explained by the extent to which the workers are structured as a group, and by reference to their past experience of struggles. To show how sabotage is part of a total history I used the results of an analysis of forms of struggle which I made in some ten new factories in France all dating from between 1957 and 1970 (Dubois, 1974a).* I was not concerned with all possible forms of sabotage, but only labour turnover, absenteeism, going slow and various types of strike; but the results of the study made it possible to present certain hypotheses about the moments when destructive sabotage of goods or machines is liable to occur.

The pattern of the different forms of struggle in such new factories is not a matter of chance. There are recognizable successive phases. In phase 1 there is no collective struggle, but there is a high rate of labour turnover and there may also be some sabotaging of machinery and goods. In phase 2 the firm is unionized, and there may be some concealment of various forms of sabotage. Phase 3 is explosive, being characterized by an indefinite strike which disrupts production badly. Phase 4: at this point the conditions exist for a number of different forms of action. This is when we find absenteeism, disputes with management which may result in reduced production, collective go-slows and the use of more planned strikes. In phase 5 the occurrence of planned strikes in some firms may be the harbinger of a return to tougher sorts of action, even of some types of sabotage.

Phase 1. Absence of collective struggles. The first acts of sabotage

The new firm starts production, the new workforce is signed on and set to work. Have they any means of protest against the conditions imposed on them, and, if so, what? Some forms of struggle are forbidden them by law, and others are objectively impossible. In France the establishment of a trade union (with the appointment of a union delegate) or of representative structures (*comité d'entreprise*, *délégués du personnel*) is virtually impossible during the first year. All candidates for representative functions must have worked at least a year to be eligible to stand; Factory Inspectors will only allow exceptions in very unusual circumstances. Since they have neither an official nor a *de facto* leadership (the workers not yet having formed into a group), the idea of a strike is virtually inconceivable, as are collective go-slows, organized resistance to management or deliberate absent-

*For a brief description of the prevailing system of industrial relations in France, see the Publisher's Preface, p. 7 above.

eeïsm. The only possible responses are individual ones, and these vary considerably. Individual absenteeism is possible, but the penalties can be considerable (agreements always stipulate a minimum time in a job to qualify for sick pay, for instance). An individual *can* argue with the boss, but is liable to be labelled for good as a troublemaker. Equally, it is possible for an individual to slow down his pace of work, but he will face sanctions and cannot depend on the support of his mates since there is as yet no solidarity among them.

In the firms where I made my study, none of these types of action was ever used during the first year. Above all, there were no strikes. Nor were regulations waived in regard to worker representation: elections were always left to the end of the first year.

Consequently, workers who are dissatisfied with their position during the first year or two of their firm's existence are reduced to making the best they can of the fact that there are always teething troubles in the early days of production (there is sometimes a certain amount of destructive sabotage at such times). Or they can choose to try and get themselves into the most desirable positions in the production line – which of course means adopting an attitude diametrically opposed to that of the saboteur. Or, finally, they can simply pack their bags and go elsewhere: labour turnover is one practicable form of sabotage during this period.

A worker can take it easy by making the most of the uncertainties of the 'running-in' period of the new work organization. Whenever a new plant or a new workshop is opened it always takes a while to get fully into gear. The pace of work is slow: the timing of each job has not yet been properly worked out, so one does one's best, and management is not too demanding. If supplies fail, or if there is a breakdown at some point in the production line, work may stop for a time. Everyone relaxes, aware that the future may be less rosy. It is pleasant to work so slowly, and the work also has the attraction of novelty – a novelty compounded by frequent transfers from one position to another during the early stages. (However, this has the compensating disadvantage that learning a new job is more tiring, both physically and mentally, than just carrying out a repetitive routine). Making the most of novelty can constitute a kind of passive sabotage: no one goes all out to speed up production. It may also be accompanied by more active sabotage: this running-in period is the time when mistakes by operators – which damage both machinery and goods – are commonest. Most are genuine mistakes, but some are surely deliberate, the aim being to prolong the easy life.

On the other hand, those workers who want to ensure the best jobs for themselves must act as anti-saboteurs. In every factory there are some departments where conditions are better, or there is an easier job to be done for the same wages. Workers sign on, of course, for a certain type of work, but in the event this can cover a number of different possible jobs. It is important to take advantage of this period before the organization has hardened into rigid compartments – before working teams have become set, when transfers are still frequent, when new sectors of production are being started up – to get the pleasantest work or to get into a team with people one likes or with foremen and supervisors who are reasonable. Similarly with the race for promotion (to foreman or supervisor): in this first period, while the firm is continually taking on more workers, there are more openings. Not all workers are aiming for this, for it means opting for tactics that conflict with the quiet-life policy: one has to get oneself noticed by one's superiors for exemplary behaviour and hard work. This means overdoing it a bit, or at least doing more than is strictly necessary.

In this first phase, then, before the workers have become a cohesive group, there seem to be two possible approaches; the two are basically contradictory, yet the same worker can switch from one to the other within a matter of weeks. Can we identify specific categories of worker as more likely to adopt one form or the other? It would seem that 'good' behaviour to achieve mobility is more common among workers with some industrial experience, people who have had one or more previous jobs. They know enough about working life to pick out rapidly the best positions and the best supervisors.

Labour turnover is not necessarily sabotage – the individual's protest against hated conditions, a way of disrupting production. A worker's leaving a firm may have no connection with the conditions prevailing there: this is especially true of young women who marry, and leave to go and find work where their husbands live, or who stop work to bring up families. However, it can in some cases be understood as the rejection by an individual of conditions laid down by the firm – the money paid, the conditions of work, the pattern of authority.

This is especially frequent in the early years of a firm (because at that stage leaving is one of the very few ways open to workers to protest). In the cases I studied, with very few exceptions, turnover rates were higher in that period than in later years. Here are a few examples: in a plant making telephone equipment, set up in 1967, the rate was 16 per cent at first, but under 2 per cent by 1973; in another plant belonging to the same company, set up in 1970, the rate was 48 per cent at first, but only 24 per cent in 1973; in a car factory set up in 1965 the rate was over 25 per cent in the early years, but fell regularly and was only 13·7 per cent in 1973; and in an electronics factory set up in 1958 the rate was over 15 per cent at first and has come down to under 10 per cent in the past few years. The differences both in the rates and in the speed of their reduction are linked with developments in the size of the workforce in each case: when large numbers are taken on at first, but gradually whittled down, the turnover rate falls fairly rapidly; when high numbers go on being taken on then the rate falls more slowly. The different rates are also related to the type of industry and the economic conjuncture.

When large numbers of workers are being taken on, selection standards are less rigorous. The firm knows that there are workers coming in who will be unsatisfactory, and in particular that some may be saboteurs. But production needs are such that there is no option. In time management will be able to get rid of undesirables: with this in view they make the training period more difficult, they manoeuvre foremen into suggesting that certain workers leave, they speed up the pace of work or produce an unpleasant atmosphere in the workshops. Thus pressure from management is also one cause of labour turnover.

The length of this first phase of the struggle varies. In most of the firms I studied it was about a year, after which a trade union would be set up. But the turnover rate often stayed high as long as large numbers of new workers were being taken on.

Phase 2. The establishment of worker representation. A drop in sabotage

When a representative body is set up, whether or not it is accompanied by a better structuring of the workers' group, the phase of reaction by individuals should in theory come to an end. Henceforward the worker can choose between a strictly individualist strategy, the individual utilization of the representative structure or its collective utilization. In all the concerns in my study the election of a *comité d'entreprise* or *délégués du personnel* always preceded the explosive phase of the first strike. After all, the calling of a strike presupposes the emergence of leaders – to disseminate information about the high degree of exploitation so frequently found in new industries – and such leaders, who in all probability began as straightforward leaders of workers' groups, will have tried at first to resolve the various problems by peaceful means. When the explosion comes it will be because the workers are protesting against the inadequacy of the prevailing representative structures or trying to establish a balance of forces which will allow them to use those structures more effectively. Sabotage is reduced (as management surveillance becomes more thorough, workers who sabotage machines or goods are dismissed): the workers now wait to see what advantage they will get from the new structures. Their disillusionment marks the ending of this phase and creates the conditions for fresh sabotage.

During this period, in all probability, the workers' group will gradually be taking shape. What are the determining factors? The shaping of the group depends first of all on the conditions described above: the preliminary period, when life is easy and workers are moving about in search of the best positions in the production process, can offer opportunities for making contacts. Yet those internal changes at the same time hinder the solid structuring of the group. The high rate of labour turnover with the resulting changes in the composition of the work-teams also militates against it. There are other factors to be considered too: where there is one training establishment, a strong bond develops among the workers who have trained together – there are not too many of them, the foremen are less authoritarian, there are longer breaks, no one is despised for their ignorance. The 'generation' of workers who trained together will, if they are not split up in the production system, constitute a solid and homogeneous group – though there is, of course, also a risk that this group may be so homogeneous as to become isolated from, or even enter into conflict with, other groups. If they are split up, all the work that went into building up the group is undone – unless the dispersal of a particularly combative group spreads the militant virus (though this is unlikely).

The type of workers recruited also helps to determine the interaction among them. A homogeneous workforce will establish relationships quicker than a heterogeneous one. In the concerns I studied, homogeneity was more usual. The workers recruited were often of the same age, the same sex and the same nationality; they also tended to have the same antecedents, that is to say, all to be entering their first industrial job.

Some factors apply more to specific factories: people brought to work by coach have less chance of making contacts after work, but tend to form sub-groups on the basis of travelling together. Where there is a works cafeteria, those who eat together will tend to form sub-groups.

Such daily routines make relationships easier. Working on an assembly-line against a noisy background can make it impossible even to converse. The total size of the workforce also makes a difference. Finally, some outside event can happen which reveals the group to itself, so to say: the 1968 strikes in particular stimulated the formation of groups in some of the firms I studied. Thus certain factors favour the creation of sub-groups (apprenticeship groups, working groups, lunch groups, transport groups, groups who work the same hours). But there is no automatic extension of the solidarity of sub-groups into the solidarity of the whole workers' group in a factory. In fact the existence of sub-groups may actually delay the formation of the larger group.

The workers' group can be quite highly structured by the end of a firm's first year of existence, when the time comes for the first election of *délégués du personnel* or the initial appointment of trade union representatives. But it may be hardly structured at all – and this is more common. It can then do little to resist the employers' strategy when it comes to setting up the system of worker representation. That strategy, aimed at forestalling the development of disputes, can be recognized from certain tactics: if management believe they can no longer postpone the setting up of a union, they decide to make the first move themselves. Their aim is to set up a structure in which they themselves can have a share – the works committee – and they support the election of candidates who do not belong to the major trade union federations, or only to such non-militant ones as F O or the C F T C; they urge all the higher grades of workers (supervisors and technologists) to attend in force all meetings of the *comité d'entreprise*, hoping that the lower grades will not be fully represented, and the higher can therefore dominate. Finally, management endeavour to influence whatever structures are set up in the direction of co-operation, giving more weight to the role of members of the *comité d'entreprise* than to the more militant role of *délégués du personnel*, stressing the importance of collaboration in the *comité* and using various strategems to sidetrack demands (rejecting certain points on the agenda, setting up investigations, referring matters to higher levels, individualizing problems).

Only a well-structured workers' group can resist this skilful manipulation by management. In the firms I studied, the strategy of the management reigned supreme. The workers in those new plants, not fully understanding how the various union federations differed, were prepared to accept whichever union was suggested, allowed incomplete lists to be put forward at elections, and finally elected delegates who were by no means representative of the workforce as a whole (skilled workers, technologists and lower management). So it followed naturally that those elected were prepared to enter wholeheartedly into the employers' ideology and its assessment of the role of the *comité d'entreprise:* they handled the spending of the welfare fund, asked for information on the running of the firm, discussed technical problems, allowed all discussions to take place in a framework of economic logic – and forgot to put forward the workers' demands.

What can the few people elected by the workers, and really representing them, do in such circumstances? How can they discuss demands within structures like these? They have very little scope. They sometimes end up by becoming fascinated with the system: they try to master the economics of the firm and use the figures they are given to base demands upon – but they often get it wrong. To succeed in making demands they need help from experienced militants who have fought battles elsewhere or from the local trade union branch.

In recent times, however, certain changes have occurred in France which make it easier to express demands through representative structures, even in new factories: a new class consciousness was created by the strikes of 1968, unions have become more firmly implanted at factory level as a result of the union recognition law of December 1968, and the C F D T has been radicalized (so that it can no longer be used to collaborate with management as it could be before 1968); and, finally, the unions now achieve more co-ordination among all the workers in a company, with militants from established factories giving advice to those in the newer ones.

As we saw, the spread of certain forms of sabotage is largely attributable to the workers as a whole having considerable control over their own struggle. Such control is non-existent in the first few years of a new factory's life: it is hard for the workers to thwart the employers' strategy of manipulating the structures of worker representation. They do not at first grasp that the candidates they have elected are failing to represent them properly, so the election of representatives marks the cessation of the various forms of sabotage. But when the scales fall from their eyes, comes the explosion – an explosion whose violence is in proportion to the extent of collaboration there has been, the degree of dependence of the union on the management and the extent to which the workers have been badly represented.

Phase 3. The explosion: sabotage by indefinite strike

In the firms in my study the phase during which representative structures were used for the almost exclusive benefit of the management was followed by an explosive phase. The explosion took the form of an indefinite strike by all sections of the workforce, controlled little if at all by the union organization, and sometimes accompanied by violence. That it was to be indefinite was not clear at the beginning. In these firms, therefore, sabotage was for the first time taking the form of a surprise strike which greatly disrupted production.

The explosion was a protest against representative structures that collaborated with management, against the impossibility of demands being satisfied within those structures, against a colluding union. In some instances it was preceded by an explicit challenge to the union in question, that challenge taking place actually inside the union branch (with new delegates confronting delegates of long standing). The challenge can take the form of setting up or trying to set up another union, which may in the end command a majority of votes. In other words, the policy of having only one union represented, which is so common in new factories, is breached in a year or two: the activists of the new union, in their protests against the earlier situation, will be the catalysts for the explosion. In other cases the explosion will draw its support from a minority union. What is essential is the existence of a solidly established kernel of militants, who either enter the existing collaborationist union, winning over the majority of votes there, or establish a new union. It is they who unintentionally unleash the explosion.

At first the explosion often serves merely to affirm the existence of a particular balance of forces. Since the structures of representation are ineffective when it comes to presenting demands, the small group of dissenting militants sets about playing its one trump card – the ability to paralyse the firm by striking. They want not an explosion but just a limited demonstration of the workers' power. The explosion only occurs when matters get beyond their control.

In other words, in the new factories I studied, the opening of the explosive phase was never spontaneous, but always fostered by militants who had come to realize – whether from observation or experience – that the existing representative structures were unsatisfactory. They would call for 'limited actions' on such points as the discrepancy between the wages in the new factory and other, older ones; but the workers on the shop floor would then go further, and turn the limited action into an indefinite strike.

So the 'explosive strike' was first and foremost an unexpected strike – even though the warning signs may have been there to see. Unexpected by the management, and unexpected by the collaborationist union, whose policy was based on there being no strike. Unexpected also by the militants. No one knew how long the strike would last; no one knew how many people would take part in it; no one knew whether all sectors of the workforce would join in; no one knew how it would develop or what forms of action might emerge. Sometimes even the demands made were quite unforeseen. A particular incident triggers off the strike, but more claims will be thrown up during the course of the action. It is this unexpectedness that chiefly accounts for the sabotage of production – by sheer disorganization.

The explosive strike is an action by the workers as a whole, primarily the unskilled but the skilled as well. Managerial staff seldom take part. In most cases the entire manual workforce goes on strike; sometimes a strike in one better-organized sector extends to the rest. In most cases, too, there is little, if any, control by the union organization. It is obvious why this should be true in the case of the assimilated union, since it is precisely against its policies that the strike is being held and, having always been opposed in theory to a strike, it is actively opposed to this one from its inception. From thenceforth it becomes clear to all that it is no longer representative, if it ever was. In the case of other unions, especially those recently set up, it may perhaps be less obvious. But even a militant union that has just won a majority of votes is not necessarily able to control the workers' explosion. Even though it is representative, it too can find itself overtaken by events. This may of course be due to its lack of experience in handling disputes, but may also mean that it has not been in existence long enough to have taken the true measure of the dissatisfaction. When this type of union includes only a minority of the workers, above all if it has not yet got any of its members elected as *délégués*, then it will itself become the means of wresting control from the larger union. Its own position is changed, especially in relation to the results of the strike: as a minority union, it will not be blamed for any possible failure, and it may even come to represent a larger proportion of the workforce.

How is this poor control by the union manifested? The length of the indefinite strike, the choice of forms of action, the possibility of violence, the priority given to this or that demand, the way the results of demands are received and the way decisions are made – all these are so many areas which may escape union control, or at least pose problems which if unresolved will cause tensions between the union and the workers. In new factories one last factor sometimes exists to explain why it is hard for the union to control the explosive strike: the fact that the militants on the shop floor may have only the most tenuous links with the local union group or branch section. In long strikes the national union federations have a moderating, if not a positively restraining effect. Certain features of the explosive strike, especially at the beginning, may be due to their absence. This kind of strike may be marked by violence, including destructive acts of sabotage: pickets which successfully impede people's freedom to work, kidnappings, occupations of the workplace. In two of the ten firms studied, there was destruction of equipment. Such radical actions, however, only appeared at a later stage. What were the reasons for them? As far as the workers were concerned, it was their first strike, and they were therefore not too certain of the dividing line between what was permissible and what was not. Sometimes only the militants knew what was legal and what illegal, but they had little influence on the strike. Thus the use of violence is another indication of a lack of any real control over developments by the union; indeed all analyses indicate that the unions work to temper the aggressive enthusiasm of the strikers. Radical action is also a way in which the group expresses itself: for the first time, the group becomes aware how strong it can be when it unites, and it wants to make the most of that strength while its solidarity is greatest. Radical action is, finally, a result of intransigence on the employers' side, accentuated (or masked) by the fact that the management of the factory concerned has very little independence, and cannot resolve the dispute without referring it back to higher levels. This often means that the strikers are never dealing with anyone in real authority – which leads to violence and specifically to kidnapping. Workers will hold a man who can make decisions and keep him, or try to keep him, until he is prepared to utter; or it may be a question of kidnapping a hostage so as to force the man who can make the decisions to come to the spot.

Does this form of sabotage pay? Results vary: on the average they are slightly better than those of strikes as a whole. But the use of tough forms of action is not the only factor in determining how a strike will end: the explosive strike is unpredictable in every way: the enthusiasm of the strikers may flag in a few days as fast as it rose, and this can happen in the very middle of negotiations – with immediate and evident effect. The union, because it has little or no control of the strike, cannot always ensure that the strikers will stick it out till negotiations are concluded. Something quite insignificant may cause them suddenly to stop believing in it, so that they give up and return to work. On top of that, the relatively low level of wages in a lot of new factories complicates matters: workers are forced back to work because they have run out of money. However, there is one final factor that increases the probability of success: the demands made are often connected with the differences between conditions in the new factory and an older one, and management finds itself no longer able to justify such disparity, and is therefore obliged to take steps to bring the two into line. After perhaps several years of taking advantage of the situation, they are now driven to agreeing to end it.

But the satisfaction or otherwise of demands is not the only result of the explosive strike. It can have an effect on the workers' group, the union militants, and relations among the union federations. The explosive strike can be the occasion of the workers' group discovering itself, becoming aware of its own existence. In several cases I was told that one of the main results of the first strike was that the workers got to know one another – something that had been made quite impossible previously by the way their work was organized. They also got to know the factory – visiting it from top to bottom, having the different work processes explained to them and trying to understand whether there was any basis in terms of work done for the different treatment accorded to different departments. What grew out of these strikes was the realization of belonging to a group, and, if the strike was a success and made the boss lose some sleep, to a strong group. This sense of belonging was often expressed by a large number of people joining a more militant union, though only for a short time.

The militants emerge from the conflict as hardened fighters; they often meet as a group to analyse what has happened and find out why they failed to control the way the strike developed. In future disputes they will be better able to hold their own. The strike is also an occasion for new militants to come forward who will provide fresh backing and reinforcement for the core of militants that in some cases existed well before the explosion.

Finally, the explosion confirms the development of inter-union relations begun during the preparatory phase. If the militant union had gained a majority before the dispute, or even some time earlier, there will be no great change: the older union will number only the non-strikers or may simply wither away, whereas the new one will take more definite shape. Where the militant union was in a minority before the explosion, the change is more marked: it will get many more votes at the next election. And in firms where no such union previously existed, one will now be officially established. In other words, in terms of unionization, the explosive stage with its three periods – preparation, strike action and immediate consequences – marks a turning point. The days of acquiescent union organization are over, and from now on there will be a union that is more representative of the working class, more prepared to make demands, and less isolated – since the explosion is often also an occasion for recognizing and therefore at least partly remedying the lack of liaison between factories in the same group.

The explosive strike is typical of a certain form of radical action. It can create the conditions for better-planned actions, and it may also lead to the use of other means of sabotaging production – such as go-slows or absenteeism. To these we will now turn our attention.

Phase 4. Multiplying forms of action. Diversifying sabotage

After the explosive phase, our analysis becomes complicated because of the variety of types of action to which workers now turn: planned strikes, the use of representative structures to make stronger demands, going slow, aggressiveness towards management, absenteeism, perhaps even a repeat of the explosive strike. Some of these can, in certain circumstances, constitute sabotage in our sense.

Absenteeism increases in firms after the explosive phase; it is always considerably higher than in comparable concerns that are longer-established. This is not only because they contain a higher proportion of the sorts of workers who are traditionally frequent absentees – women, young people, unskilled workers, the unmarried. It is also an expression of individual protest against a situation which there is no way of changing collectively.

In France, when a factory is new, when a lot of people are still being taken on, when a large proportion of the workers keep leaving, when the average worker has not been there long (often less than a year) – a stage that may last for two, three or four years, depending on the firm – then the majority of the workforce will not qualify for monthly salary status. The few lucky ones who do can stay away from work, but not the others; if they do, they will only receive day-to-day Social Security payments, so they hesitate before staying away. In the very first years, then, the absenteeism rate in new factories tends to be low. Absenteeism is not a viable option, since the individual will lose not only his earnings but also his credibility with his employers: it will not help him to be labelled a slacker.

On the other hand, once the worker has been there for some time and feels more sure of his position, absenteeism becomes a possible individual response. All the trade unionists I spoke to about absenteeism said that it was due to working conditions, fatigue, payment by results, monotonous work and poor relations with management. So one hypothesis is that the higher absenteeism in new factories is a means of protest against the way the workforce is exploited there.

A second hypothesis as to why absenteeism is so common in new factories is that here is a group of workers with no industrial traditions. I do not mean this merely in the obvious sense: what I mean is that a large proportion of the workforce have not interiorized the behaviour patterns of industrial society. They do not take work or output for granted, hence they do not come to work because they do not want to. A manager explained this in terms of laziness; a trade unionist put it in other words: 'Why kill yourself working for a boss when you can have a few days off for nothing?'

A third hypothesis about absenteeism in new factories relates to its increase after the explosive phase – especially if that has been a failure. The workers have tried to change their situation collectively by striking; when that fails, the possibilities for collective action are reduced for some time afterwards; people therefore look to individual action as all that is left. In several of the factories studied, I was told that absenteeism had increased significantly after the explosive strike.

Disputes with management can also disrupt production badly. Absenteeism cannot be a collective form of action: if it becomes collective (if a whole work-team or workshop stay off work) then it is doomed to fail, for it becomes unauthorized absence and the absentees are penalized. A dispute with management, on the other hand, can be an early form of collective reaction. At an earlier stage, before the explosive phase, managerial staff are perceived by the workers in a new factory as different from themselves: they are likely to have been recruited from another factory, rather than from among local people; they are recruited before the other workers, and are thus senior to them in the firm, and on average they are also older; often the manager is a man when the majority of the workers are women. Because they are different, they command obedience; even if they are despised they are not directly defied. Furthermore, since the workers as a whole are not yet organized, they cannot conduct a collective dispute. They fume inwardly, but only the bravest actually express a protest, and they are disciplined.

But there is often a great deal of dissatisfaction with management among workers in a new factory. Though the first tensions may come from the mere fact that they are different, it is chiefly the style and content of their orders, their poor work organization and their technical incompetence that will give rise to confrontations. In almost all the firms studied, reorganizing the pattern of authority figured as one of the aims (if only implicitly) in the explosive phase. Negotiations in this sphere were often unsatisfactory, and after the return to work it continued to be a problem which might easily become the object of direct action by workers.

Such direct action is not generalized, and it always appears after the explosive phase. It is easy enough to see why – the demand has been expressed, and their participation in the explosion has given them a new awareness of their strength and solidarity as a group. They can now struggle collectively against things they dislike. Once they stop being afraid, direct action against authority starts with a change of attitude – you no longer lower your eyes when the foreman looks at you, but look him boldly in the face. Then comes deliberate infringement of all the manifold regulations of the firm: people talk or sing at work, everyone goes to the toilets at once or without permission, they stay there longer than usual, they take longer break-times or hang around the vending machines; if the foreman tells you off, you say, 'I'll see the *délégué* about this.' In some of the new factories we looked at in our study of strikes in 1971, we found other forms of reaction: a collective refusal to obey, or preventing the management from controlling the flow of work. However, direct action against a specific pattern of authority, or a particular climate of authority, remains fairly restricted in scope and one does not find it everywhere. The group must have developed an awareness of its own strength; the strike must not have been a total failure; the management must have opposed the strike and behaved in a vindictive way afterwards in an effort to reassert their temporarily discredited authority; they must form a group who are still alien to the workers (i.e., not many workers must have been promoted as foremen); and they must not yet have become practised in the modern, 'human relations' approach to giving orders. Also, for this type of action, the workers must be able if need be to get support from the union, which is not always easy with a new union that has only been established since the strike. It is also always a temporary response, depending on there being a balance of forces favourable to the workers – which is an uncommon situation. Solidarity can flag after a period of being keyed up; similarly, the management can recover their self-assurance.

Collective go-slows are also a temporary form of action, since they too depend on there being a situation favourable to the workers – always very short-lived, since managements have disciplinary means available for bringing it to an end. The generic term 'go-slow' includes the various forms of action described in Chapter 1. In each case the aim is to reduce production below the target set or hoped for by those in charge. In almost all the firms studied, some form of go-slow appeared after the explosive phase – a reduction of the collective pace of work, an appearance of activity with little real work being done, work left unfinished – which considerably disrupted the normal production line.

By all these various forms of action, workers were trying to achieve more than one type of aim: they wanted to extend the time allotted for particular jobs either because they were too hard, or as a means of raising their earnings or grading. Sometimes the two objectives were combined. And we found one case when workers who had up to then been paid by the hour were changed over to piecework, and operated a go-slow in protest.

What are the conditions that give rise to this type of action and enable it to succeed? In every instance in which it occurred, the collective go-slow followed the explosive phase. It sometimes appeared immediately after the explosive strike, as a consequence of its partial failure (workers who have failed to get satisfaction from an indefinite strike try fresh forms of action); it also appeared as an independent movement, unrelated to other actions; it appeared, finally, as the precursor of another strike – the dispute would begin with a go-slow and later expand into a total strike.

The main reason why the go-slow generally follows the explosion rather than the other way round is that going slow calls for a well-organized group to manage it, and before the explosive phase the group is not usually very formed. But before we analyse this basic factor, we may note the incidence of several secondary factors which determine the practical form the go-slow will take. It must depend on the way production is organized whether it is based on individual productivity, or an assembly-line; it will depend on the way wages are related to output (whether payment is by time or by productivity). Obviously it is easier to operate a go-slow when you are paid by the hour and when individuals are working independently.

However, the prime factor is the capacity of the group to organize this type of action. They must understand the work process well enough to know the most effective way of slowing it down – the aim being to see that the boss loses more money than the workers do. In one plant the worker representatives took several years to discover the decisive importance of the way earnings were computed: beyond a certain level, earnings rose only half as fast as production, so going slow should consist in reducing the pace of work until that level was reached, thus causing the employer to lose twice as much as the workers. Other points to be considered are the visibility and the extent of the disruption that will be caused by the method chosen. The decision to go slow and the choice of how to do it are never spontaneous; they presuppose there being a leader – a trade union militant or a political activist – with experience of such action in other factories to draw upon. He plays a decisive role both in suggesting the method and in putting it into operation, but the choice must be a collective one, since group unanimity is an essential prerequisite for success.

The group must then be sufficiently united and organized to

be prepared for the inevitable counter-attack by management and to stand up to it. The go-slow happens at the work-bench, and the foremen on the spot are the first to try to stop it by putting pressure on individual workers, especially those they judge to be the weaker members of the group. Then follow threats of sanctions or perhaps actual sanctions (pay stoppages, suspensions, dismissals). In most cases, a go-slow is juridically illegal in France, so those responsible may incur legal penalties, but not always (it all depends on the terms of their contracts and the payments system). The group must be solid enough to stand up to threats, and to prevent defeatism in their own ranks – for defeatism is the sure first step to defeat. The group may not have realized quite how much repression they were incurring – for instance there was one group of apprentices who operated a go-slow under the influence of a left-wing militant while still in training. Because they were still on trial the management could sack them, and they had no support from the other, trained workers, for the simple reason that they did not know them.

Thus, it takes an organized group to analyse the situation, choose the most suitable technique of going slow and stand up to the pressures and sanctions it will have to face. All this is easier after the explosive phase: by then people have got to know one another, and have formed groups. The workers will know who in their own group is likely to succumb soonest, and can act accordingly. Their cohesion is also greater because the composition of the work-teams becomes more settled after the first year or two: work organization has come to a more or less routine stage, earnings systems are fixed, changes within the plant are fewer, not so many people leave: consequently the group will have been together for some time, which is one of the main conditions for cohesion.

The instances of go-slows in my study were seldom effective by themselves; most of them only had partial success, the workers failing to carry their action through to the finish because of the threat of sanctions, because they were insufficiently prepared or because of counter-moves by management (such as shifting the people concerned to other departments). A go-slow aims at achieving certain visible objectives, but by its very nature it is also a way of contesting authority, and in this sense is related to forms of action discussed earlier. It also becomes a challenge to the prevailing organization of work – far more so than a strike, in fact, for it affirms control by the workers over their own work, precisely the control that the prevailing organization of work seeks to deprive them of. It is often more disruptive than a straightforward work stoppage.

Absenteeism, insubordination towards authority, going slow: none of these exclude the possibility of *striking*. In every firm there will be a lot of strike action after the explosive phase. What are its characteristics? When does it happen? In what form? Is it controlled by the union organizations? What does it achieve? The first strike after the explosive strike is in a sense related to it. If the explosion has been partly, or completely, successful, the first strike follows fairly quickly. If, on the other hand, the explosion has ended in failure, the first strike will occur much later. In other words, if the workers have won they are eager to try again; if not, they are reluctant to launch a further venture. It then becomes much harder for the trade union to get another action started, even a mere token stoppage. The result of the explosive strike also determines the nature of the first strike that follows it: if success, then the first strike will be a limited one, but, if failure, then another explosion is more likely. This is the opposite of what one would have expected: one would think that workers encouraged by victory would have no hesitation in throwing themselves into another all-out strike, in the hope that it would be equally successful. But in fact the success of the explosive strike is accompanied by a reinforcement of trade union control, and this tends to channel dissatisfaction into the more sophisticated and elaborate forms of action that are only possible where the union is powerful. If, on the other hand, the explosive strike has been a failure, then the conditions that gave rise to it remain. As soon as the stormy atmosphere builds up again, the explosion will recur: and a weak union, weakened further by the first explosion, can do nothing to stop it. Thus, when the explosive strike has been a success, there may be further strikes quite soon, but they will take a more institutionalized form; when it has been a failure, it will be longer before there are further strikes, but when they come they are more likely to be explosive again. In the first case production is not greatly disrupted, whereas in the second it is.

Overall the propensity to strike is more developed in the post-explosion than in the pre-explosion phase, except when the first explosion has been a failure. The explosive strike may mark the advent of a period of more frequent strikes – in some firms, indeed, there are major strikes every two or three years. In such cases the explosive strike has led into a phase of intense struggles appearing at regular intervals.

This post-explosion period is a time both of varied forms of action and varied forms of strikes: there may be indefinite strikes by the entire workforce, indefinite strikes by one category of workers or one workshop, repeated short stoppages by the entire workforce, repeated short stoppages by one workshop or one category of workers, or a series of general stoppages which later develop into indefinite strikes.

As for trade union control, that now varies much more from one strike to another than it did in the previous explosive period when it was always weak. In the few recurrences of explosive strikes, the situation is similar to the one described above. We discover three new patterns of union control: it may be extensive, disputed or limited. Where there is extensive control, the union handles the strike from start to finish; in agreement with the workers, it chooses the demands to be made, the moment for striking, the length of the strike, the nature of the action; in some cases the union has to take complete charge because the workers are not sufficiently organized. But union control, or control by one union, may be disputed. One must remember that the explosive strike has often increased union membership. During an explosive strike workers object to the decisions, or lack of decisions, of the union; in later strikes the situation is rather different. In general one organisation will tend to hinder the development of strike action altogether, while the other will tend to extend it as widely as possible. In practice tensions may arise over certain aspects of the strike (the use of illegal forms of action, how long it lasts, the setting up of a strike committee, the demands being made, the organization and timing of voting, the running of workers' meetings). The third pattern, limited control by the union, tends to emerge when there is a strike by one workshop or one category of workers: where there are relatively few workers involved, they can manage their own affairs; all strike decisions are taken collectively, perhaps with the *délégués* for that section if there are any. The union as such controls the extension of the strike to other workers or other workshops, an extension the strikers may or may not want to see. These fresh strikes may bring about further trade union divisions or cause votes to shift from one federation to the other in the next elections.

The explosive strike is often limited to the new plant; it only makes sense in terms of the new situation. Later on, however, the workers in the new plant can start to take part in combined action with other factories in the same company. Such action is related to setting up the equivalent of combine committees, but it is not usually initiated by the new workers, who are content to follow a lead from elsewhere.

How do the employers react to these further waves of strikes? Works managements are no longer caught unawares: since planned strikes are announced ahead of time, action can be taken against them. This may take the form of technical re-dundancy or more punitive action against strikers than during explosive strikes. As for management resistance to demands, the strikes of this period are rather less effective, because employers are better prepared: 25 per cent end in success, 25 per cent in compromise and 50 per cent in failure.

During this post-explosion phase, too, there may be more theft, either in reaction to lack of success in the first all-out strike, or in protest against an exploitative situation. If the boss doesn't want to pay a fair wage, we'll take what he owes us direct. This type of action remains a minority one, but sometimes it is organized. In one ten-year-old plant, three years after a violently explosive strike, ten workers were sacked for thieving: they had set up a regular system for selling shoes and boots stolen from the company.

In new factories the explosive phase is followed by a phase of multiple forms of action – individual (absenteeism, theft, insubordination) and collective (go-slows, planned strikes, further explosive strikes). This variety is natural, corresponding to the increased complexity of the situation inside the plant. The position of the workers in the company's established plants remains objectively different from that in newer ones: in the former, traditional forms of action are appropriate, but in the latter there is always the possibility of another explosion. Another factor that leads to a variety of actions is the establishment of one or more cohesive groups in a plant: a workers' group that is very closely knit because the members have always worked together and are not much affected by changes inside the plant, can resort to such varied actions as go-slows, organized resistance to authority and planned strikes. On the other hand there may be one workshop in that same plant where the workers are quite disparate – perhaps the workshop where new employees always start. There one will find mini-explosions. So a multiplicity of forms of action is also an indication of the diverse composition of the various workshops. In a few years' time, the life of the new plant settles into a routine; in particular, the work organization gains a certain stability. Because there are fewer changes, the workers are better able to judge what can be done in any given department at any given time. Finally, and above all, the major factor in explaining the multiplicity of forms of action seems to me to be how the plant becomes unionized after the explosive phase. A better-organized union can see that the workers deploy their efforts more efficiently, varying them from workshop to workshop, from trade to trade, from one set of circumstances to another; the aim is to maintain an almost continuous level of combativeness and agitation, which, though it may have less startling successes than those won by the explosive strike, makes more lasting and progressive gains. The multiplicity of forms of action may also to some extent result from competition among the union federations, a competition which did not exist before the explosive phase when, at best, only one militant union would ever be present. Coordinated union effort (which the union of a new plant can take part in after a few years) also accounts for some types of action: planned strikes affecting all, or a large proportion, of the plants in one company, stoppages of a few hours recurring at more or less regular intervals.

In short, after the explosive phase the climate of dissatisfaction is maintained more steadily, but is markedly less virulent. However, in plants where the explosion was a failure in the workers' terms, the conditions for a sudden and violent upheaval may easily recur within a few years.

In new plants, then, the workers' struggle goes through successive stages, whose duration and intensity vary from place to place. The fact that collective struggles are not possible at first partly explains the behaviour of individuals in trying to pick out the best positions, staying for only a short time, sabotaging machines or goods. Then a representative structure is set up, but at first this simply operates to integrate the workers into the company's system. Their objection to the way this structure works, their objection to unrepresentative delegates and their electing of more militant delegates may all be signs that the third stage of the struggle is about to start – the explosion. That third phase is followed by one in which the forms of action are considerably diversified – absenteeism, organized resistance to authority at every level, go-slows, theft, limited or indefinite planned strikes (which may extend to all employees or only the blue-collar workers, to a few workshops or a few trades) and further explosive strikes: any or all of these types of action are possible.

Any comparison between forms of struggle in the new and in the well-established plants in a single company must be seen in the framework of these stages. The factors that account for the multiplicity of forms of action in new factories after the explosive phase (working conditions, the structuring of the workers' group, the stabilization of production and of work organization, the various types of trade union activity) are also present in the older-established plants. Logically, one would expect to find the same multiplicity there. But, in fact, because unions so often tend to settle down into a routine, we sometimes find a fifth stage, consisting exclusively of planned strikes, when sabotage no longer occurs.

Summary

To our question, 'Who are the saboteurs?', Friedrich Engels's reply was that the workers' movement was a movement of saboteurs at one point in its history, before it became organized into trade unions. At the beginning workers would steal and destroy, but later on, supported by the trade unions, they began to use strikes as a means of making demands. Finally they came to see that they would only succeed in improving their condition by way of the political struggle to take over the state power now held by the bourgeoisie. Saboteurs are barbarians; sabotage was the youthful sin of the workers' movement.

But sabotage is still with us; it subsists alongside strikes and other more political forms of action. Who, then, are the saboteurs? Are they the workers whom increasing industrialization has recently thrust into factories? It would seem that these new categories of workers – women, young people, ex-farmworkers, immigrants – are not necessarily any more given to sabotage than certain groups of skilled workers. So the lack of industrial and trade union traditions is not the only reason. Are they the workers who occupy strategic points in highly automated industrial processes? If such workers take the risk, they can cause tremendous damage; but we also find saboteurs in mass-production industries, and even in firms where production organization is still at a primitive stage. It does not seem, then, that workers become saboteurs because of the type of workers they are.

More convincing, I think, is the hypothesis that sabotage spreads in consequence of the workers on the shop floor having more control over the form their industrial action takes. The great strike movements in the late sixties contributed to the winning of such control by workers. In France the trade union organizations came to terms with the new situation, and have since then allowed more autonomy to their branches in individual firms. That independence of local branches may account for certain of them deciding to resort to tough forms of action which seem suited to their particular circumstances.

In fact, I would conclude that sabotage depends not so much on the history of struggle in the workers' movement as a whole as on the cycle of struggle in the individual firm: in the factories where I was able to make a detailed study of the history of disputes, I found that there is a tendency for labour turnover and some destruction of machinery and products to precede the start of an explosive strike that disrupts production badly; this tends to be followed by other types of sabotage – absenteeism, theft, go-slows and sometimes further explosive strikes. A group of workers who are not at present resorting to sabotage may have done so in the past, and may again in the future. The success or failure they have had in earlier experience of disputes is the determining factor: the Pechiney workers decided in 1973 that they would stop carrying out safety precautions on the electrolysis tanks because of what had happened in 1968. They had then wanted to save their equipment, and had kept the aluminium furnaces alight so that they would not be damaged, perhaps past repair, by a long period out of use; however, the management had failed to revise the grading system, as the workers had demanded. And even in 1968 the strikers had gone further than ever before, by sabotaging the aluminium bars they were producing, deliberately making them defective. Similarly, the Lip workers only succeeded in setting up such varied and complex forms of sabotage because they had a long experience of struggle behind them.

Thus, to understand the appearance of sabotage in any firm one must know precisely what phase in the cycle of disputes it has reached, and to what extent the workers are structured *as a group* (how cohesive it is, whether it is still taking shape, whether it has been defeated as a group, whether there is a really active minority, whether there are several different competing union organizations, how strongly unionized they are, whether a new union has recently been set up).

Finally, we come to the part played by management: the employers may well be provoking sabotage by the policy they are following; they also seek to find solutions for it.

5 Sabotage and the Employers

An employer in Lyon in the last century decided that one form of sabotage – idling – was due to wages being too high. The cure was clearly to reduce wages: 'To ensure and maintain the prosperity of our industries, it is essential that the working-man should never grow wealthy, but should have only just what he needs to be well fed and clothed. With a certain class of people, too much affluence stifles industry and breeds idleness, with all the vices that flow from it' (quoted in Moissonnier, 1975). This employer considered that the workers' attitudes were to some extent dependent upon him; if he changed his own behaviour, then he might hope to change theirs.

Of course not all employers carry this view to quite such ridiculous lengths. But we must consider the responsibility employers have for workers' sabotage, and analyse their reactions when confronted by it. In Chapter 2 the responsibility of management was implicitly suggested: workers are reacting against a specific situation created by management, but the demands they formulate may in fact have nothing to do with it. We must now analyse that situation directly to discover just how far management can be held responsible. The organization of work, the pattern of authority, a refusal to recognize trade unions – all these things can account for sabotage, as can the stance taken by management during a strike. Workers are actually driven to sabotage by their employers.

But the employers do not then sit back and watch: all sabotage produces a reaction, in two phases. There is the immediate reaction – in most cases one of repression: physical repression, sanctions or legal action. Then there is the longer-term reaction: this again may be one of repression (changing regulations to make them more repressive, setting up a more authoritarian system of management). Or it may involve reviewing policy more fundamentally: the employers adopt a new economic policy, a new personnel policy, a new policy towards the unions, in general a policy whose aim is to deal with the underlying causes of the sabotage. I shall be laying special stress on present-day moves to formalize industrial conflict, because they are among the most sophisticated ways of preventing disputes from becoming radicalized – yet they have still failed to stop the spread of sabotage. I will finally conclude this chapter by describing the ideological offensive that accompanies these reforms of policy: every action to restrict production is met by a speech highlighting the benefits of growth.

Management responsibility

In the first half of the nineteenth century we find a somewhat surprising apparent contradiction: workers responded to the introduction of mechanization by breaking the machines, yet in the biggest of all workers' rebellions of the period – the Lyon rising in November 1831 – the weaving looms were spared. But the contradiction *is* only apparent: in most cases the workers no longer owned their own machines, but at Lyon the master-weavers, who whipped up the revolt in the first place in order to get a minimum price recognized by the dealers, still owned theirs – and they would hardly have wanted to destroy their own property. So sabotage is first and foremost a result of the capitalist system, of the fact that the means of production are in private hands; the worker who no longer owned his tools no longer had the same respect for them. Only the influence of socialist ideology has brought workers back to a respect for their working equipment: do not destroy today what will be yours tomorrow. Nevertheless, those who commit sabotage today still say to themselves, 'These machines are not mine, these goods are not mine, these premises are not mine – so why should I care about maximum production?' The prime responsibility for sabotage rests with the employers simply because of the fact of their ownership. That is so obvious that we may be in danger of forgetting it.

The introduction of a technological change can be the occasion for sabotage: Luddism was initially a response to the introduction of machinery into the textile industry; dockers in England today systematically slow down their work to counter the effects of the modern process of containerization (Wilson, 1972); the dispute at the *Parisien libéré* in 1975, when the workers decided unilaterally first to cut down on the number of copies printed, and later to destroy them all, was also a response to new printing techniques. By modernizing, and by dismissing workers and bringing existing benefits into question, the management were taking a risk: the responsibility for this sabotage was theirs.

The division of labour, separating the planning of work from its execution, the fragmentation and repetitiveness of certain jobs – all this can drive people to sabotage. F. W. Taylor discovered this from bitter experience when he introduced his principles of scientific management. He believed this would cure some forms of sabotage for which the employer was to blame: in his view the workers had been idle because the firm allowed them to be; their work was wasted because of inefficient work methods. But in fact, after he brought in his methods, the workers broke their machines to prove that the pace he wanted to set them was crazy. And control systems of this sort still drive workers to revolt, as R. Hess tells us:

Everything is done to deprive workers of the use of their intellect; both machinery and foreman are there to tell the worker to shut up and stop thinking, that thinking is unnecessary and even dangerous. The worker enslaved to the assembly-line or the machine must be isolated. He must cease to be aware of what is happening. Rebellion then builds up against this de-humanizing situation [Hess, 1974].

It might in fact seem that authoritarian methods which deprive the worker of all responsibility would be bound to give rise to sabotage, as a kind of demonstration whereby the worker wins back some degree of control over his work. But this is not what one employer thought in 1830 – in his view laxity was the root of all evils:

All too many manufacturers have found their business going badly solely because they have so forgotten themselves as to lose all dignity and authority by over-familiarity with their work-people. Once there is no longer any respect or fear, then it is not long before the idea of cheating their master comes to them, and the wish to do it follows: they start by cheating in unobtrusive ways, by stealing time; then small things start disappearing; and as one thing leads to another, there comes a day when they do something that can lead them to prison or worse [Bergerie, 1829-30].

Methods and rates of payment decided upon by the employer can also lead to sabotage. As we saw, F. W. Taylor considered that one of the chief causes of idling by workers was piece-work; contrary to what one might expect from such a system, the worker did not work faster in order to earn more. If he worked fast, he thought, the boss would only reduce the rate paid for each item produced, so he worked slowly to keep the rate steady. This attitude can still be found today among workers involved in the hand-rolling of steel: they work slowly, since if the present norm were to rise, that might lead to a review of piece-rates (C. Durand, Prestat and Willener, 1972). It has also been said that giving monthly status to workers previously paid by the hour so that no one loses money because of illness has made absenteeism increase. Finally, the kind of reduction in rates of pay common in the last century can lead to sabotage: the go-slow by Hungarian workers which we looked at earlier followed a cut in wages (Hethy and Mako, 1971).

Sometimes it is a policy of production at all costs that is responsible for sabotage. In 1873 workers at the Vienne trade fair complained that more and more badly made goods were being produced: 'If shoddy work is the rule, it is because of too much division of labour, and because the institution of apprenticeship has fallen into disuse.' Nowadays, too, workers complain that they are being forced to waste materials or make products of poor quality: in a cooked-meat firm, the workers are expected to keep up a certain pace of production, however wasteful it may be. The management say: 'It doesn't matter if you leave 200 grammes of ham on the bone; all that matters is to bone the hams quickly and produce the number required.' Similarly in a shoe factory: 'One must produce without worrying about quality. Working so fast is bound to result in mistakes: a shoe without a tongue, two left shoes in one box. The boss says duds don't matter – he just wants so many pairs of shoes' (quoted in Dumont, 1972).

The risk of sabotage can be enormously increased by a refusal to recognize that workers have common interests and a consequent refusal to accept any organized workers' representation. Here again the responsibility lies with the employer: in France the Le Chapelier law of 1791 and the Allarde decrees of 1803, which outlawed workingmen's combinations, opened the door to goods being sabotaged (products of high quality disappeared, skimping became the norm). Lengthy strikes – a form of sabotage which seriously disrupts production – were reduced once trade unions were recognized as a valid means of negotiating. Shorter and Tilly find this the sole explanation for the decline in strikes with violence against persons and property in France after 1920: the employers agreed from thenceforth to negotiate on a regular basis with a 'strong and formalized union organization'. The refusal to recognize trade unions can provoke worker sabotage, but, as we shall see, recognizing them does not necessarily cause it to disappear.

Finally, we must not forget the responsibility of management for some instances of sabotage during strikes. Sabotage is in fact commoner in defensive strikes, when the boss initiates the dispute by deciding to suppress an established right, to dismiss or transfer workers or to change the wage system, the organization or conditions of work. This was true of the strikes between 1871 and 1890 (Perrot, 1973) and is true of strikes today (Dubois and Durand, 1975). In these cases, it seems as though the workers unconsciously make excuses for themselves: 'The boss attacked us first, so he must have been waiting to see whether we'd react.'

Sabotage during a strike can also be a response to violence by management. In the 1877 railroad strike in the U S, 102 locomotives, 2,000 carriages and a station (Pittsburgh) were destroyed following a violent confrontation in which twenty people were killed (Brecher, 1972). In our analysis of the 1971 strikes we also found that in a not inconsiderable proportion of those strikes (about 25 per cent), management repression was the immediate cause of strike action being intensified and moving towards violence.

To sum up, then, the responsibility of management for worker sabotage can be direct or indirect: direct in certain strikes, and direct when an established right is brought into question; more indirect when it takes the form of a change in policy (the pattern of authority, rates and methods of payment, work organization). To refer to the private ownership of the means of production as being responsible for the appearance of sabotage may seem to be merely a matter of form; however, it is the essential starting point from which all else follows.

Repression

When an employer is faced with sabotage his first reaction may be to make concessions and satisfy the demand being made (cf. Chapter 2). But he may decide on repression, and that can take three forms: it may be bloody, disciplinary or penal.

Bloody repression means no holds barred: force is opposed by force. The Luddites who broke machines in early nineteenth-century England rapidly found themselves confronted by armed resistance – both from regular soldiers and from strong-arm men paid by the employers. There were violent incidents, and numbers of people were killed and wounded. At Anzin in France in March 1833, in the 'four *sous* strike', pickets stopped work, the boiler fires were put out, the galleries began to be flooded, the coal lay on the ground and the miners would not allow it to be loaded onto the barges, barrows and shovels were thrown down the shafts and machinery was broken. Troops were called in and charged the crowd, wounding a large number. In France during the Second World War the Germans responded to sabotage with a policy of taking hostages, and a number of them died. Since 1968 a number of workers have been killed in the course of industrial disputes, either by the police or by security forces directly employed by the management.

Disciplinary repression is a perfectly legitimate response on the part of an employer, because he is the owner of his plant. He can therefore penalize workers for sabotage. For instance he may fine them: F. W. Taylor recounts how, when machines were deliberately broken in protest against his efforts to achieve greater productivity, making the man in charge of a damaged machine pay for the damage stopped the machine-breaking. Such financial retribution is still to be found today, in Sweden for instance: the blueprint for industrial democracy that is under discussion at present stipulates that the worker bears responsibility for any damage to installations or machinery caused either intentionally or as a result of gross negligence (*Intersocial*, no. 4, April 1975). Absenteeism, too, is dealt with in financial terms, with bonuses for regular attendance. The most usual thing is for disciplinary repression to work through a system of graduated sanctions: a verbal warning to the offender, then a written one, suspension, transfer to a different workshop, dismissal with or without notice and with or without compensation. The seriousness of the punishment is tailored to the seriousness of the offence.

In 1830 people were dismissed for ordinary absenteeism (Bergerie, 1829–30). In September 1948 there was an attempt to counter absenteeism in the mines by decreeing that 'Any worker who has been absent without justification for six successive days, or for twelve days in all in any period of twelve consecutive months, shall be considered to have given in his notice and be struck off the payroll.' A look at the history of strikes shows occasional mass dismissals: in the period 1871–90 employers sometimes reacted to any work stoppage by issuing dismissal notices. After the time stipulated, absentees were held to have resigned (Perrot, 1973). Then there were the massive dismissals of railwaymen and postal workers after the strikes of 1909 and 1910. More recently, in 1971, 16 per cent of the largest strikes ended with the dismissal of the strikers – though it was sometimes more politely described as the non-renewal of temporary contracts (Dubois and Durand, 1975).

Penal repression is inflicted by courts of law. Saboteurs may be made to pay fines or damages, or given prison sentences which may or may not be suspended. Between 1825 and 1864 almost 10,000 people were sent to prison in France simply for having gone on strike, and 150 of them were in prison for over a year. Between 1865 and 1896 another 5,000 strikers were gaoled. But this is rare today: in 1972 the court of summary jurisdiction in Caen passed suspended sentences of from one to eight months on some workers who had locked up their foremen – but that was not actually sabotage. On the other hand, prison sentences are still usual when there has been sabotage involving the destruction or theft of machinery or goods. One of those responsible for deliberately ruining equipment at the Brandt plant in Lyon in 1971 was given a five-month sentence, two months of which were suspended. However, in 1890 the demonstrators who stole a length of cloth on the May Day demonstration in Vienne were sent to prison for from one to five *years*.

Not all sabotage meets with repression; if the employer does not prosecute, if the two sides prefer to settle the dispute with an agreement which excludes legal action, then offences in theory punishable by law remain unpunished. But, in addition to the repression that actually takes place, we should be aware of just how much repression is possible. Here a brief historical survey will show the direction in which legislation and jurisprudence are moving.

Destructive sabotage – of machinery and goods – is subject to fines and prison sentences. As early as 1810, Article 443 of the French Penal Code dealt with punishments for damage to merchandise and anything used in its manufacture. In any period when sabotage increased there was always a tightening up of the laws in force. After the anarchist outrages of the 1890s the legislation of 1894–5 was passed (the '*lois scélérates*'), whereby not merely was destructive sabotage itself criminal, but also any sanctioning of it; people could be punished not only for the act, but even for belonging to a group which was likely to commit the act. During the last war the Germans went even further: in September 1940 they started by putting up notices in every post office to the effect that 'any damage to means of communication – telegraph poles, cable box connections, post office equipment – is prohibited on pain of death'. The quasi-insurrectional strikes of the autumn of 1947 also led to a stiffening of the law, the further '*lois scélérates*' of 6 December 1947, whereby any act of sabotage ('destruction or damage to any machine, equipment, plant or installation') was liable to ten years' imprisonment or a fine of anything from 2,000 to 1,000,000 francs. These laws were abrogated in February 1948. The violent leftist demonstrations, the 1968 strikes and the various acts of sabotage in the France-Dunkerque yards certainly helped to provoke the next law, passed on 8 June 1970 to cover new forms of delinquency: all instigators, organizers or deliberate participants in any concerted action to destroy or damage goods could be punished by a prison sentence of from one to five years. Shorter sentences might also be passed on any instigators and organizers of gatherings who did not give the order to disperse as soon as they discovered the destruction or damage. Furthermore, those responsible for the damage must pay to make it good. This last law is still in force today.

Theft was dealt with in Articles 379, 384 and 386 of the 1810 Penal Code – articles which make clear the class discrimination embodied in the Code. The mere fact of belonging to the working class constitutes a reason for making all penalties more severe. Article 386 stipulates five to ten years' imprisonment as the punishment for theft committed by 'a worker, journeyman or apprentice, in his master's house, workroom or shop'. The heaviness of the penalty is explained by the fact that in addition to the theft there has been an abuse of confidence – confidence bestowed by the master and betrayed by the worker! In 1974, a deputy asked for the repeal of this article, so reminiscent of the days of serfdom; he suggested, in 'compensation', the introduction of stronger measures for dealing with thefts from large stores, where 60 per cent of all theft is by the staff. It goes without saying that those who sabotage machines or goods, or who steal, can be dismissed without notice or compensation.

Since the beginning of the nineteenth century, French legislation has been consistent in condemning destructive sabotage and theft; all that varies is the scale of the penalty. But this is not true of strikes. Up until 1958 the history of the right to strike was primarily one of increasing liberalization: the Le Chapelier law of June 1791 prohibited combinations either of employers or workers, permanent or temporary (i.e., during strikes), and any infringement of this law was liable to penal sanctions. This apparently equitable law was, however, far more stringent for the workers; from 12 April 1803 the penalties for workers (a month in prison) were stronger than those for employers (a fine, with imprisonment as an option). The law of 27 May 1864 made combining no longer a crime – strikers were no longer liable to penal sanctions – but it was still a crime to interfere with anyone else's freedom to work; furthermore, a strike broke the work contract, and the employer was not obliged to re-employ a striker nor, if he sacked him, to pay any compensation for unfair dismissal or dismissal without notice. The right to strike was formally recognized again by the 1946 constitution, and again by that of 1958: 'The right to strike is exercised in the context of the laws regulating it.' The last liberalization came in 1950: after the Dehaene stoppage it became clear that civil servants and all those employed in the public sector have a right to strike; the law of 11 February 1950 stated that 'a strike does not break the work contract except in cases where the employee is seriously at fault'; an employer who dismisses strikers as such is guilty of unfair dismissal. However, the last twenty years have shown a trend towards increased repression: the right to strike of public broadcasters was restricted, and it was denied altogether to certain airline workers; the law of 31 July 1963 restricted the right to strike in the public sector; the law of 3 June 1970 (the so-called '*loi anticasseurs*') was designed to repress further types of offence.

This brings us to consider how matters stand today in regard to the repression of sabotage-strikes, strikes which materially disrupt production: lengthy indefinite strikes, strikes disrupting some part of the production process (bottleneck strikes, spreading strikes, selective strikes) or strikes in which people are prevented from getting to work (by pickets or by occupation of the premises). The indefinite strike is not illegal. However, this general rule is subject to one exception – it does not apply in a case of re-quisitioning. Under the National Service Law of 1938 strikers can have their right to strike removed by a straightforward requisition order (as happened on 13 July 1938, 7 January 1959, 21 July 1962) which can be issued where there is 'a threat to any part of the national territory, any sector of the national life or any sector of the population'. Disobedience to a requisition order is punishable by up to a year's imprisonment and a fine. There was frequent requisitioning in the early years of the Fifth Republic, but there has been little since then. It is interesting to see how other countries have legislated for this same problem. Some articles of the Taft-Hartley Act of 1947 in the U S deal with strikes which could endanger the national economy. They allow for the President to appoint a committee of inquiry to examine the problems at issue. He can then ask the competent court to forbid the strike for a maximum of eighty days, after which it becomes legal again.

In France bottleneck strikes and spreading strikes are illegal if they represent a concerted plan to disrupt production. But it can be quite hard to prove that a concerted plan exists. Most legal judgements have condemned this type of strike, but there is in fact no penal sanction attached to it. The law of 31 July 1963 explicitly prohibits spreading strikes in the public sector, yet this did not stop public service workers, especially railwaymen, from reverting to the practice after 1968.

Until recent times strikes with picketing and occupation of premises were always considered by the courts to be illegal, since they interfered with the freedom to work – an offence according to Article 414 of the 1864 Penal Code. 'Any person who, by use of force, violence, threats or deception, shall cause or uphold, or endeavour to cause or uphold, a concerted cessation of work, with the aim of enforcing a raising or lowering of wages or of preventing the free exercise of industry or labour, shall be punished by imprisonment of between ten days and three years, and/or a fine of from 500 francs to 10,800 francs.' Occupation has also been declared illicit by the courts, since it infringes the rights of private property. Backed by this law, the employer can ask the court for an injunction requiring the strikers to leave, and can call on the police to enforce it. However, some more recent judgements lead one to suppose that the occupation of work premises may one day become a licit means of exercising the right to strike. In the Rateau case in March 1974 the magistrate, instead of granting an injunction, looked into the reasons for the occupation and insisted that the two sides negotiate. The judge in the high court of Grenoble went even further in April

1974: he refused to expel the strikers, on the ground that in this instance the occupation was not impeding anyone's freedom to work. It was of course infringing the private property rights of the employer, but there was no serious risk attached: 'The safety officers have been given access to the factory.' Will occupation become a right, as long as it causes no damage and impedes no one's freedom to work? The appeal court in Grenoble did not think so, for it quashed the previous court's judgment. In this case the occupation was not really sabotage at all, nor did it prevent non-strikers from working; it did no more to stop production than a stay-at-home strike would have. Yet the strikers were penalized for picketing and/or occupation by being dismissed without compensation.

In Great Britain the law does protect strikers, who cannot be arrested simply for participating in a stoppage. There were attempts at the end of the last century and the beginning of this to reduce the protection afforded to strikers by the repeal of the Combination Laws; and the Taff Vale case in 1901, when the owners of the Taff Vale railway successfully sued the Amalgamated Society of Railway Servants for damages after a strike, was a severe setback. However, a powerful protest movement led to the reversal of the Taff Vale decision and the right to peaceful picketing was restored in the 1906 Trades Disputes and Trade Union Act. The Act also protected unionists against actions for civil conspiracy.

Except for the two world wars, when striking was illegal, the only piece of anti-union legislation this century before 1971 was the 1927 Trade Disputes and Trade Union Act, which outlawed sympathy strikes. It was repealed by Labour in 1946.

The situation was relatively stable, then, between 1906 and the beginning of the 1960s when the development of unofficial strikes saw new attempts to limit strike action. The return to power of the Conservatives in 1970 and the passing of the Industrial Relations Act of 1971 brought severe restrictions with the establishment of the Industrial Relations Court. Unions were expected to register with the Registrar of Trade Unions and Employers' Associations, but the TUC strongly advised their members not to register and to boycott the Court. Its 1972 Congress actually suspended thirty-two unions which had failed to comply with these instructions.

The Industrial Relations Court had the power to impose a cooling-off period and require a secret ballot to be held in serious disputes. Also illegal under this law were mass picketing, go-slows, working to rule and overtime bans. The Court could impose fines on unions which engaged in 'unfair industrial practices' and could also order them to pay compensation. However, apart from a few important and damaging cases, the Act did not have an unduly adverse effect on the unions. Employers had little recourse to the Court, and even before the return to power of Labour in 1974 it appeared that employers preferred co-operation with the unions to open conflict.

Perhaps the most famous case to be brought before the court was that of the 'Pentonville 5'. In 1972 dockers ignored a court order to stop the blacking of vehicles using the Midland Cold Storage Company. As a result five dockers were jailed for contempt. This led to a national dock strike and the release of the dockers after a few days through the intervention of the Official Solicitor.

Labour were returned to power in 1974, and in the same year the Trade Union and Labour Relations Act repealed the Industrial Relations Act. It reaffirmed the right of unionists to peaceful picketing for the purpose of obtaining or imparting information and for persuading. The Act does not protect the picket against prosecution for related activities which are themselves unlawful and which might occur on any picket line, such as obstruction; there was a notorious use of the charge of conspiracy in the case of the three Shrewsbury building workers gaoled in 1974.

There was further cause for alarm amongst trade unionists when, in the increasingly strained industrial atmosphere of 1977, the Criminal Law (Amendment) Act entered the statute book. Several of the provisions of the Act are regarded as having severe implications for the movement, in particular with regard to occupations and picketing. Workers are now exposed to the liability of arrest for criminal trespass in the event of an occupation, and any failure to co-operate with the bailiffs who are evicting factory occupiers is now a criminal offence.

What about the repression of forms of sabotage whose practical effect is to reduce production? Working to rule is a legitimate practice. There is no way of penalizing people for working without enthusiasm, for constantly changing jobs or for refusing to go into industrial jobs. As for those who prefer to remain unemployed, they are likely to find their unemployment benefit cut off if they refuse too many suitable jobs offered them by the Labour Exchange. This leaves us to consider what repression there is for going slow and absenteeism.

In France going slow is not a legitimate form of action. The Supreme Court of Appeal's social division has made this clear several times: working at a slow pace or with deliberate interruptions (when output is disrupted, when people rest for a quarter of every hour for instance) does not constitute a strike. Hence when there is a go-slow 'the parties are still subject to their contractual obligations, and the worker who is dismissed without notice or compensation for contravening instructions to return to normal production cannot protest against his dismissal on the ground of his right to strike'.

One employer in 1830 advised that Monday absentees be dismissed out of hand (Bergerie, 1829–30). Nowadays the repression of absenteeism is rather more complex: the worker who is absent without any reason and stays away for more than forty-eight hours will be reprimanded; if he does it again, he may be sacked. It is more difficult when the absentee is provided with a token medical certificate. It is easy enough for the worker to bring an accusation of unfair dismissal. Management has to adopt a twofold tactic. The first thing is to make it financially profitable for people not to stay away from work, by reliability bonuses – but with paid sick-leave these do not always achieve their aim. (This has led many people to question the whole principle of monthly salary status.) A second tactic is now coming into use: doctors are employed by the management to visit the homes of the absentees and check that they really are ill. However, there is strong union resistance to this idea.

Are the various forms of sabotage being repressed effectively? The recent spread of such tough kinds of action would lead one to think not. Repression of absenteeism is a case in point – as can be seen from two studies carried out in British companies. At General Motors (Scotland) management twice stepped in in vain to try to stem the overall rise in absenteeism: in 1970 they adopted a system of issuing warnings to workers who were regularly late or absent without medical certificates. The number of one-day absences without any excuse went down, but this was accompanied by an increase in the number of one-day absences *with* medical certificates! In 1974 management set about trying to cut down on absences where the medical certificate was not genuine: six workers were sacked and others threatened with the same penalty. But, again, this action was only effective in the short term (Behrend and Pocock, 1976).

The General Motors study was of male employees only; but the second study was of women, and the results were very similar (Nicholson, 1976). In the second case the firm had a very generous system of sick pay. Finding that the increase in absenteeism was becoming extremely expensive, management decided to take action in 1971: they drew up a list of absences over the past fifteen months, issued warnings to all who had been absent more than five times, and actually dismissed eight employees. What followed was a change in the nature of absenteeism: short absences became fewer, but long absences increased and, while few people were now absent without a medical certificate, more people were absent *with* one. The workers soon adjusted.

The author of this latter report suggests that less weight should be given to the system of medical certificates; it is better to trust people to tell the truth about their own sickness – and there are examples to suggest that this has a favourable effect on absenteeism rates. On the other hand, the ineffectiveness of prevailing means of repression has led to demands for stronger means of repression, with sabotage condemned more unequivocally and the right to strike more strictly regulated. However, the use of penal sanctions against saboteurs who destroy machinery and goods, workers who steal and strikers who impede the freedom to work is not just a matter of law and jurisprudence. It is also largely conditioned by the balance of power between boss and worker: if the employer wants to preserve an atmosphere of harmony in his firm, it is not in his interest to seek repression; on the other hand, if his aim is to defeat the saboteurs at whatever cost, then he will resort to the force of law. Disciplinary repression, too, is related to a balance of power – even more so indeed – since if it is used in response to a strike, it generally results in a further demand being made (for sanctions to be lifted) and thus usually leads to prolonging the strike. In such cases it is clearly useful to turn to some strategy other than repression – which is a more sensible approach, since it attacks the root causes of the sabotage.

Working out new policies

The employer who wants to get rid of sabotage considers what intelligent measures may be used in preference to brute repression. The solution is obviously to do away with the occasion for the sabotage, to strike at the causes of it, by introducing new policies: new techniques, a new policy of work organization, a new earnings policy, a new pattern of authority, a new employment policy (later on I shall come to the question of policy towards trade unions).

The use of more sophisticated techniques is a traditional way out: automation cuts out the risk of human intervention and its attendant errors, and thus the risk of sabotage to the product. It also removes the opportunity for going slow, since the worker can no longer interfere in the process to lower production – production is done by the machine, whose pace of work is fixed by someone else. Finally, doing away with individual hand-held tools reduces the risk of theft: a worker operating a computer-controlled machine tool has not got much chance of stealing it – and, in any case, what could he do with it if he did? On the other hand, technical improvement does not get rid of the risk of sabotage by negligence: a machine can go wrong, and if the operator does not report it the damage may be considerable. It is possible for workers in the most modern plants to let the machinery sabotage itself, so to say, without much risk of being found out; breakdowns are common enough, and it can be quite hard to discover the causes. Technical improvement therefore solves nothing; it removes some possibilities for sabotage, but creates others.

The employer can also change the work organization in his plant, thus resolving several of the problems posed by sabotage. He can set up new workshops – repair workshops first of all, which deal with the sabotaging of goods in the course of production. When not too much damage has been done, the product can be saved with a bit of touching up. Since the routine of the other shops must not be disrupted by giving the job of re-touching to the shops where the defects arose, special new repair departments are set up. In all mass-production industries they are kept very busy. New workshops, or even whole new factories, can also be set up to counter another form of sabotage – the 'bottleneck' strike. Some departments play a key role in the production process, and a stoppage in them results in paralysing it in both directions (not only is further production stopped, but because there is no room to keep any more half-finished goods, production higher up the line has to stop as well). The only solution is to avoid the possibility of a bottleneck by making sure that this is not the only workshop of its kind: the same component must be produced in two different workshops in two different factories, and it is then to be hoped that they will not both go on strike at once. This is a gamble that does not always pay off, especially when it is only done on a small scale – if a single assembly-line is replaced with two smaller ones next to each other, for instance, the risk remains.

A way of trying to cope with sabotage caused by going slow is to place selected workers at crucial points in the production process. This is a very old management tactic: Pouget gives an instance of it from the turn of the century, when building contractors made a point of employing one really robust worker on every site to stimulate the others. Anyone who did not follow his example would be shown up, and laid off as not strong enough for the job. One finds employers doing the same sort of thing today. What happens, for instance, when a new assembly-line starts turning out lorries? To begin with there is no regular flow of work, and the tendency is to move slowly so as to prevent too rapid a norm being set. The youngest and most skilled are therefore put at the beginning of the line; all the workers are placed with a view to getting the best quality production out of them. Later on, once production is well established, it is quantity that is all-important, and the most docile workers are placed at the head of the line: they will set the pace, and those further down have to follow them. Obedient workers will not go slow, and will make it impossible for those who follow to dawdle unnoticed. But this only works for a time: if the group is organized they soon manage to make their more zealous colleagues see reason (Bernoux, Motte and Saglio, 1973).

Another tactic is to change the division of jobs. In the past the idea was to fragment work as much as possible, so as to reduce the power wielded by skilled workers over production. Since they were irreplaceable a strike by them really was sabotage; mechanization, and the replacement of skilled with unskilled workers, solved that problem. When unskilled workers went on strike, they could be replaced at a moment's notice from the dole queue. In the US, for instance, in 1892 the steelworkers' union – to which all the skilled workers belonged, and which therefore held an impregnable position – called a strike. But after several months of confrontation, they lost: Carnegie made no concessions at all and, what was more, he mechanized his factories so that he could employ only unskilled labour, people he could dismiss and replace at will (Brecher, 1972).

Today, on the other hand, an answer has been found to the sabotage that arises from lack of interest (spoiling goods, slow working, absenteeism, working without enthusiasm, the flight from industry) in 'job enrichment'. This takes various forms: workers can be moved from one position in the production line to another, jobs can be enlarged (several operations formerly carried out separately being assigned to a single worker, with the cycle time doubled or trebled), or they can be made more comprehensive (letting all workers do a certain amount of repair-work and checking, for instance). However, the most interesting experiment of this kind is the setting up of autonomous or semi-autonomous production groups: such groups are responsible for a certain proportion of a firm's output – the quantity and quality of production, their own work organization and the upkeep of the machines; they have a certain money allowance for a specified time (usually a month) and a financial stake in the results achieved; if they fulfil the terms of the contract they get a bonus. Therefore, if there is any sabotage the whole group is penalized: if machinery is sabotaged there will be more breakdowns and more time spent on maintenance work; if products are sabotaged then quality requirements will not be met; any striking or slowing down will affect the quantity produced. The group are in a position to commit sabotage, but they will hurt themselves by doing so, since they will fail to fulfil the contract they have signed. The autonomous group is thus the best way of countering all the various forms of sabotage; analyses have shown that it also leads to a lower rate of absenteeism and job turnover. The French national agreement to improve working conditions signed on 17 March 1975 is in line with this, envisaging as it does autonomous production teams: 'Depending of course on the technical limitations, it appears that setting up teams with a certain amount of autonomy contributes to enabling wage-earners to take part in their own work organization and to developing their capacity for initiative.'

Sometimes the ground can be cut from under the feet of would-be saboteurs by a reform in the pattern of authority. This can be done in one of two ways – by greater authoritarianism or greater flexibility. In 1830 an employer recommended greater strictness as a way of preventing go-slows or the sabotaging of tools and goods; silence should be the rule in all workshops. 'Permit no conversation: talking is the occasion for much wasting of time or, worse, it causes distraction and leads to the spoiling of tools or materials. It has been found that there is a lot of conversation where the two sexes are together. It is therefore a sensible arrangement to separate men and women whenever the organization of the work permits' (Bergerie, 1829–30). Increased supervision, spying and intimidation, introducing among the workers management agents whose sole function is to keep an eye on them – all these are authoritarian methods which seek to repress sabotage by force. But the employer who has used fear for some time will only find the revolt worse when it comes. A more intelligent tactic is to relax management control in order to reduce the amount of sabotage: where there is less pressure of authority the worker no longer wants to take it out on his implements or the goods he is producing. The recent trend towards setting up small production units instead of vast industrial prisons shows a similar approach: if the place they work in is on a human scale, the workers are bound to feel more at home in it. If they feel at home, then it feels more as if it is their own place – and they will hardly want to damage it. In factories of this kind everyone knows everyone else, and the saboteur has no hope of being lost in the crowd. In such firms, in fact, it is to be expected that sabotage will be reduced because the workers are more closely supervised – no longer in an authoritarian manner, but a paternalistic one.

A classic remedy for sabotage is to provide financial incentives. These may be negative: fines, having to pay compensation for damage done or money lost, a reduction – or abolition – of the reliability bonus. Or they may be positive: workers can find it pays them better *not* to commit acts of sabotage. Reforming wage systems may take contradictory forms. In 1910 F. W. Taylor concluded that piecework payment was a cause of go-slows ('systematic soldiering', he called it): workers keep their production below a certain level for fear that if they work faster to earn more, the employer will simply lower the piece-rate; therefore the piecework system must be abolished, and instead a standard of production fixed, with workers who do not reach it penalized. Pouget, writing at the same period, said the opposite: French employers, he said, to get rid of slow working, introduced piecework payment instead of payment by the hour. Clearly, the employers were largely feeling their way in the dark. Perhaps the main object was to change things so as to disconcert the workers, but it did not take them long to adapt to the new method of payment: Pouget says that reducing the quantity of work would then be succeeded by reducing its quality. Earnings were then – and are still – manipulated so as to persuade the workers to produce the maximum quantity or quality: output bonuses to individuals or teams, monthly or yearly productivity bonuses, quality bonuses, profit-sharing schemes, etc. The monthly salary status agreements made in France in 1970–71 have often been interpreted as an attempt to attract into industry a labour force that preferred to seek work elsewhere, in the tertiary sector. There is thus good reason to describe it as an attack on the sabotage of refusal to work in industry. But it has led to a rise in absenteeism.

Employers can deliberately manipulate employment policies and timetables to deal with a form of sabotage like absenteeism: in recent years it has gone down in firms which have continuously reduced staffing levels and also in firms where working-hours are cut. Fearing to be the next to go when cuts have to be made, workers in these firms are reluctant to admit to being ill; they think that absentees will be the first victims in any mass lay-offs (Dijkstra, 1974).

A final remedy for the 'allergy to work' found not only among young people but also among adults is to give everyone equal opportunities for time off, for leisure and personal fulfilment. This is based on two things: on the one hand, 'there is, in man, a natural need to do freely chosen work to establish his identity. That need can only increase as his level of awareness rises, and will be diversified as his understanding of the world develops.' This idea leads to the attempt to counter people's allergy to work by the use of such modern methods as autonomous production groups. On the other hand, there must also be leisure, to give greater freedom: 'Progress will never free man totally from the obligation to work, but it will give him ever greater opportunities to satisfy his needs for action, creativity and fulfilment – always provided that what he does at work is not his sole and indispensable means of fulfilment and satisfaction' (Rousselet, 1974).

To sum up, then, these various technical, organizational and policy changes are not all equally effective in removing the workers' temptation to sabotage production. Some of them merely remove the possibility of one kind of sabotage while opening the door to another: this is the case with technical progress and with changes in methods of issuing orders or computing earnings. Only certain organizational changes, such as the total re-definition of people's job-content and working environment by the introduction of autonomous groups, are likely to be totally successful – and then only if the workers are prepared to cooperate, which cannot always be guaranteed. We turn next to the attempt to formalize industrial conflict by recognizing the function of the trade unions in industry and making the most of systems of negotiation: this represents a major onslaught on the current wave of sabotage.

The formalization of industrial conflict

Over the past ten years, in all the west European countries where I have been able to make a comparative study (Dubois, 1974b), management has reacted to the increased radicalization of disputes (especially since the waves of strikes of 1968–70 which were on such a scale and of such a length as to cause real disruption of production, and thus sabotage the economy) by a greater formalization of industrial conflict. Indeed, that seems to them to be the object of these strikes, which were in effect attacking the inadequacy of industrial relations at company level. The degree of formalization has certainly risen during the period. But once again new forms of sabotage have arisen to meet the new situation (fresh strikes, tougher and more diversified measures, direct action).

What is meant by the 'formalization' of industrial conflict? Formalization exists when the system for regulating conflicts of interest functions smoothly. This presupposes several conditions: a pyramidal negotiating structure (national inter-industry level, national trade level, regional or local level, and company level), and an organization of the two sides (management and unions) at each of these levels. The government is also an interested party: while recognizing the full freedom of both sides to negotiate, it can define the principles, lead the way itself in the public sector, give financial assistance and extend and generalize the scope of certain agreements. The two parties must be recognized as being competent to negotiate – in other words, to discuss the problems of those they represent – as well as having freedom of expression and organization (in the workplace as well as outside it). The ideal is to arrive at a right of co-decision, with decisions made on the basis of a consensus.

The system functions well if each of the organizations, especially the union, is established on principles of 'democratic centralism'. This means that the representatives are democratically appointed for a specific period (not just a specific negotiation) and, once elected, are empowered to bind those they represent for as long as the agreement stipulates to block strikes and to discipline any of their members who step out of line. An agreement should cover all matters relating to work conditions, and should include clauses allowing for the use of conciliation machinery in the event of differences over the interpretation of its terms; it is also desirable that it have a built-in adaptability to all possible changes, especially those in the economic situation (allowing for a sliding scale of wages, for instance).

The system also presupposes a certain consensus as to ideological aims: it rejects class conflict and rests upon the principles of economic growth (based on technological progress and industrial peace) and a fair distribution of the fruits of that growth. These principles in fact underlie a number of programmes and projects known by a variety of titles: the welfare state, workers' participation, Capital–Labour co-partnership, social planning, the new society, incomes policy, progressive agreements, the social contract, productivity agreements, etc.

For there to be formalization, not merely must the union (or unions) be organized and recognized, but they must also accept the hierarchy of authority, the terms of the agreements, the underlying ideology. Consequently certain conditions make formalization easier: the existence of a reformist trade union movement that is unified and centralized, some representation of the Left in government, political stability (a government with a solid majority and no major internal conflicts) and economic expansion.

Even when the system is fully established and all these favourable conditions are present, there are still certain inescapable danger spots and danger periods. The first problem is the

competence of the various levels of negotiation (should everything be debated at all levels, or should there be a certain
specialization?). Secondly, there is the fact that agreements come
to an end. The re-negotiation period can produce a hardening on
both sides, and the overall consensus as to aims may shatter
into fragments. Finally, the system has from time to time to face
the problem of changes in representation: during political
elections, the authority of the government is reduced, and the
same is true of union leaders during union elections.

Of the countries I studied (France, Great Britain, Germany,
Italy and Belgium) in the period before the first wave of strikes,
obviously none presented a perfect model of the formalization
of industrial conflict. But some were closer to it than others.
The first industrial crisis can be interpreted as being a reaction
to the inadequacies of the system, and it usually develops at
company level, since in all countries this is one of the weak
spots of the system.

Formalization before the strikes of 1968–70

The degree of formalization achieved varies from one country to
another, but in all of them we find favourable conditions beginning to take shape – notably the coming to power of the
reformist Left.

Formalization seems to have reached its highest point in
Belgium: national inter-industry agreements on social planning
have been in existence there since 1960; there is an impressive
list of national bodies on which the unions have a voice; high-
level tripartite meetings are frequent. There are over fifty
management/union committees at industry level. At company
level there are certainly fewer; however, union delegations and
councils function and are accepted everywhere. The union
federations are powerful: the Socialist and Christian federations
form a common front when it comes to presenting demands,
meeting to agree about what claims they will make before
negotiations begin; they assert their independence of the political
parties, but their ideas converge with those of the Social Christian–Socialist coalition in power at the time of writing. They take

part in the system of decision-making in Belgian society as a whole. Since 1960 they have actually become stronger: in 1963 the first collective agreements restricting benefits to union members were signed. The industrial relations system works via a delegation of powers – at the moment when agreements are signed the rank and file are not consulted. Agreements run on average for two years, make explicit reference to industrial peace, and stipulate that in case of dispute there must be arbitration and conciliation. They are gradually coming to embody more and more provisions for raising workers' living standards – a third week's paid holiday, for instance. The whole system is in line with the ideology generally described as 'social planning'. In Belgium, then, formalization is very advanced, but there remain two weaknesses – relations at company level, and the extreme rigidity of agreements.

By the end of the period studied, the German system had come very close to the Belgian; around the middle sixties several things happened which helped the (already considerable) formalization to increase further. In 1966 the SPD (the Socialist Party) came to power in coalition with the CDU (Christian Democratic Union) and CSU (Christian Social Union). In 1967 the national trade union federation, the DGB, agreed to act in concert with the government. In 1968 the SPD set up a trade union council which was to take part in working out the economic and social policies of the party. Also in 1968, the unions consented to sign agreements that would run for longer. There is strong formalization of industry-based negotiations in Germany, especially at regional level; union organization is structured around some ten powerful, rich and highly centralized industrial federations. Higher up, on the other hand, at national *inter*-industry level, formalization is not very advanced; to start with, power is shared by the SPD with other parties, and in fact the DGB as such has little authority over its affiliated unions. At the lowest level the company is both a strong point in the system and a weak one. It is strong, because there are structures for class collaboration at this level: the famous 'co-determination' system in mining and steel gives an equal voice to management and workers on the supervisory boards of their firms, and a labour manager appointed by the workers' representatives is on the board of management. In other industries there is no such parity on the supervisory board. In every firm a works council is supposed to collaborate frankly and freely with the employers; though it has a certain control, its members, who are elected by the workforce as a whole, must by law be independent of the trade union. But the weakness of the system at this level is the absence of the trade union as such from the workplace: its trusted agents on the shop floor, its local sections, have no *legal* existence at all. Furthermore, at this level there is no clearly defined negotiating structure: industry-based agreements may be adapted to suit a particular firm, but there is no guarantee that workers will receive any other advantages that may have been conceded. As in Belgium, the negotiators can sign agreements and are not responsible to the workers; agreements last for eighteen months on average; industrial peace is taken for granted; appeal procedures run smoothly. At the top formalization is considerably behind what it is in Belgium: this is largely due to the fact that the SPD were in opposition until 1966. Since then it has been able to develop in much more favourable conditions, given the strong links between the SPD and the DGB (many people belonging to both, deputies belonging to trade unions, consultations over plans, etc.). There is no ideological problem: in 1959 the SPD had adopted a welfare programme which abandoned all idea of planning and nationalization, and in 1963, at its congress in Düsseldorf, the DGB followed suit.

In Great Britain the formalization of industrial relations, which is more or less second nature to the British trade union movement, was showing signs of petering out in the early sixties. The most obvious manifestations of this were the development of wildcat strikes and the failure of joint consultation procedures. However, an opportunity arose to breathe new life into the system without having to go through a major social crisis, when the Labour Party won the general election of autumn 1964. The traditional links between Labour and the TUC (subscriptions, trade union MPs, Labour participation in the TUC and TUC participation in the Labour Party conference) should have made reform possible – and there was certainly no ideological barrier, since the British trade unions did not want revolution. The reforms – or the attempts at reform – were to centre upon who took part in negotiations and at what level, and involved an attempt to reconsider a whole series of restrictive practices on the shop floor. The Donovan Commission was set up in 1965 to provide for a wide-ranging discussion on these matters. At national inter-industry level, where there was as yet no formalization, there was a first attempt to bring the parties together in August 1966 (at a conference on wages and salaries); this gave birth to the National Prices and Incomes Board. That same year it was decided to create a new national employers' organization, the CBI. Consultation also continued during the work of preparing the draft of the White Paper, *In Place of Strife*. At the level of the different industrial sectors of the economy, where the most important agreements were supposed to be negotiated, there was chaos. In every sector there was a proliferation of unions (unions for different skilled workers, for different industries, general unions, white-collar unions: demarcation disputes were endless); on the employers' side things were no better, and not all firms belonged to the CBI.

The Donovan Report of 1968 recommended a simplification of structures and a federation of trade unions similar to the AUEW. There was negotiation at company level, but it was not formalized: in theory the employer was supposed to deal with the secretary of the union's local branch, but there could be thirty unions involved in a single industry. In practice the negotiator for the workers was often the shop steward, who represented the workers but held only a minor place in the union. Shop stewards became everyone's favourite target for attack, since they were held responsible for the wildcat strikes.

The first step to reform was the policy of productivity agreements: this was designed to control restrictive practices by workers (supported by the unions) which seriously hampered the growth of productivity. Working conditions had to be changed so that more was produced, but without any increase in costs (the wage concessions offered to workers to get them to agree to the changes were made up for by reducing costs in other areas, for instance by cutting down on overtime). This met with little success – very few such productivity agreements were concluded. The Donovan Report and *In Place of Strife* also suggested certain changes in industry, which would tend towards a greater formalization of disputes: union power should be reinforced (the right to certain information during negotiations, the appointment of representatives to some management boards, recognition of a union in every firm, guarantees against unfair dismissal, the right to appeal to outside arbitration); and at the same time regulated through formal procedures governing, for example, methods of applying industry-based agreements, the regulation of disputes within the firm, the rights and obligations of union representatives. These reforms did not in fact come into operation under the Labour government; in exchange for certain concessions to the unions (linked also with the aim of controlling wages) they wanted a stricter regulation of the right to strike – directed specifically towards preventing wildcat strikes. The TUC opposed it: the law was never passed, and the TUC promised merely to put pressure on their members, a promise that was worth little in view of the fact that the shop stewards were largely outside union control. Thus, despite its having begun so hopefully with Labour coming to power, the period 1964–9 was marked by the failure of the attempt to intensify the formalization of industrial relations.

In Italy, unlike Belgium, Germany or Britain, formalization was not supported by a reformist ideology in the unions. The largest organization, the CGIL, has a clear anti-capitalist orientation written into its constitution. Thus formalization has had to fight its way against ideological opposition, but it was assisted by the setting up of the first centre–left governments in 1962. The history of negotiation in Italy is one of progressive decentralization, though with no rejection of the negotiating levels already in operation: after a period of highly centralized negotiation, the right of separate trades to conclude agreements was won around the mid-1950s and of individual firms to do so in 1953; the largest union confederation, the CGIL, gave its approval in 1957, and at last in 1963 management conceded over piecework systems, job evaluation and work organization. In the early sixties all three levels of negotiation existed; the unions were greatly in favour of agreements covering particular categories of worker (i.e., trades) being dovetailed with the agreements concluded in individual firms. Agreements were given a definite time limit, quite a long one (three years on average), and there was an appeals procedure. All this tended towards formalization, but there was no legislation covering the right to strike. Everyone admitted the legitimacy of negotiations at company level (there was much less repression of union activists), but this was undoubtedly the weakest link in the system: the recession of 1963–5 held back its development; the *commissione interne* (factory committees) and workplace union sections were moribund or at best stagnant; worker/management works committees set up from 1966 on to settle differences over productivity deals, though consisting of representatives of the workers concerned, were appointed by the regional union organizations. Thus there was plant-level negotiation but no plant-level union organization really controlled by the workers as a whole. Though there were strides made in formalization over the period, it was far from complete by the time the strikes began in the 'hot autumn' of 1969: the ideology of the C G I L was still revolutionary, the right to strike was barely regulated by law, and union organization at plant level was totally ineffective.

In France, as in Italy, the formalization of industrial conflict immediately came up against an ideological problem: the C G T, the majority union organization, openly advocated the class struggle, and the anti-formalizing tendency of the unions was reinforced during the period. In 1964 the C F T C (French Confederation of Christian Workers) became the C F D T (French Democratic Confereration of Labour) and abandoned all reference to Christian social ideas. Confronted by this kind of ideological orientation, the government endeavoured to introduce a new ideology favourable to formalization – workers' participation. The Left alone would have had any hopes of success in getting such an idea accepted, of perhaps persuading the unions to adopt it – but the Left were in opposition. Only the two minority unions (Force Ouvrière and the C F T C) took up the idea of participation, and it soon came to mean no more than profit-sharing.

In juridical terms France was furthest ahead in formalization. The three types of agreement (national inter-industry, industry-based and company-based) were all possible (though not all could deal with the same issues). However there was a general slowing down of negotiation, and no inter-industry agreement had been made since 1958; company agreements were few and far between; the only agreements that progressed fairly steadily were at industry level (national, regional and local). Union organizations were not recognized as such by companies, the *comités d'entreprise* existed to cooperate with management and the job of the *délégués du personnel* was merely to see that laws were enforced and agreements implemented. There was no formal arrangement allowing workers to negotiate improvements in terms and conditions at plant level: either they had to use the existing consultative machinery as best they could, or they had to rely on the union organization outside the firm. Nor was there much formalization of the results of negotiation: agreements, which usually ran for an indefinite period, were negotiated without the workers concerned being consulted and did not inhibit them from striking for better terms, the lengthy appeals procedures never being used.

Thus the overall system of industrial relations was not greatly formalized, though efforts in that direction saw some progress during the period. What is most surprising is that the first approach should have taken place on the ideological plane of workers' participation. At the same time, the power of the union organization outside the workplace was reinforced. A first attempt at tripartite meetings was made in 1963, with the incomes conference. That same year the right of public sector workers to strike was restricted. From 1965 onwards there was a stronger move towards formalization: men who favoured negotiation came to the head of the employers' organization, national inter-industry negotiations on employment were started up again, and the government encouraged negotiation in various ways. However, the workplace still remained outside the formalizing process: the obligation laid down in 1967 to establish profit-sharing agreements only resulted in intensifying antagonisms, and union meetings were still not allowed in the workplace. In any case, the institutionalizing moves of 1965–7 were taking place in an economic context of recession which considerably hampered their chances of success.

The strikes of 1968–70

In all these countries, then, industrial relations became gradually more formalized during the sixties, but nowhere did this reach the ideal outlined above. The workplace was still the weak link in the system everywhere, either because real issues could not be negotiated seriously there in any systematic way, or because the union, which should have been the worker's advocate in such negotiations, was not recognized as having a voice.

The strikes of 1968–70 therefore appeared in the guise of a wave of disputes with individual employers, controlled little if at all by the union organizations, which had no official power on the shop floor. Obviously, they seemed like anti-formalizing movements (there were criticisms of the underlying ideology from left-wing fractions in the unions and from extremist groups), yet they also represented a criticism of the lack of formalization at company level.

In Belgium the strikes were primarily a criticism of the system from within: protests against the extension of agreements, against the absence of any clauses enabling them to be adapted to improvements in the economic situation, against industrial peace clauses, against the exclusion of the rank and file from any control of negotiations. There were protests because the demands of the rank and file were not being heard: either there was no system for putting them forward in the workplace, or they fell outside the category of claims open to negotiation, or they were transformed into mere wage-demands that could be seen as fitting into the logic of the system.

Like the Belgian, the German strikes of 1969 sought to update the whole system of industrial relations: safeguards for the benefits already won in particular companies, a possibility of altering clauses in an existing agreement if the economic situation improved, the setting up of a formal system whereby workers could express their demands within their firms – a system that could deal with those problems of work conditions not dealt with, or not adequately dealt with, at other levels of negotiation.

In Great Britain the strikes that occurred in industry after the withdrawal of the Labour government's plan for improving trade union rights and restricting the right to strike were not so much a protest against an outmoded negotiating system at the lowest level as a show of strength in order to preserve power already won. The control exercised by workers in certain spheres – for example, through the restrictive practices discussed in Chapter 3 above – had been directly assaulted by productivity agreements. Strikers were protesting, too, against wage controls (abandoned in June 1969) and the limitation of the right to strike. In other words, the industrial strikes in Great Britain were definitely directed against formalization, since the existing rather chaotic situation allowed of greater control by workers than would be possible under a more formalized negotiating system.

In Italy the election of strike committees in the strikes of autumn 1969 (but also from the end of 1968 onwards), the role played by workers' assemblies, the struggle over demands worked out by the rank and file – a battle waged to the bitter end without any sign of compromise – combined to demonstrate that the struggle was centred on the weakest point in the system of industrial relations: the workplace, in other words the level where the day-to-day demands of the workers, which were not merely related to wages, were not being passed on. In some firms the criticisms voiced were more fundamental, challenging the whole process of formalization then taking place; this was especially true where left-wing political groups were involved. But we cannot say that the unions simply travestied the aims of the strike movement by making use of it to formalize their presence on the shop floor; the very form of the disputes (throwing up delegates and assemblies) indicated the crying need for a structure of worker representation to present demands at plant level.

In France in May and June 1968 the tripartite centralized negotiations at Grenelle, which took place during the course of the revolt, increased the formalization of industrial relations: merely by taking place they constituted a 'summit' negotiation, not exactly an everyday occurrence. Furthermore, they led to recognition of the right of unions to organize within the workplace, though bargaining rights at company level were not conceded. The fact that the strikes continued after these negotiations leads one to think that the strikers were not going to be satisfied by their movement's being used merely to fill the gaps in the negotiating system. There were some speeches about self-management, which suggests that the movement was also directed to a certain extent against formalization. But this tendency towards a more fundamental opposition to the system could not develop in the absence of revolutionary theory and significant political forces which rejected the electoral game. The second part of the May movement was therefore also obliged to make a contribution to the process of formalization, mainly at trade and company level.

Formalization since 1970

The first waves of strikes in 1968, 1969 and 1970 led to a reinforcement of the process of formalizing industrial relations. The union organizations tried to stimulate the combativeness of the rank and file as part of their strategy, to stiffen their power at the point where it was weakest – at company level. Government and management had learned their lesson from the period of intense conflict: they too would speed up the formalizing process, either by using strong measures to enforce further restrictions on the right to strike (so that conflicts of interest would not result in open war), or by letting the unions play a greater part, or, finally, by launching a great ideological offensive – with a whole new vocabulary – to give fresh currency to less radical ideas.

The waves of strikes also gave the workers' movement a new vision of its own strength: that strength could be used to modernize the formalization of industrial relations, but it might also serve to prevent it. The fact that, after the first waves of strikes, forms of struggle became increasingly more radical and new types of sabotage appeared indicated a trend against formalization, confirmed in some cases by a resurgence of revolutionary ideas among sectors of the workers' movement.

Formalization could be reinforced harshly: it might be hoped that if the right to strike were withdrawn or restricted, would-be strikers would turn to peaceful methods for reconciling disputes. But repression and the use of force are of doubtful efficacy, since they may well produce the contrary of the intended effect, by hardening the position of those against whom they are used. That is presumably why the strong hand was not used everywhere. We have seen what the effects of repression were in France after the strikes of 1968–70. In Great Britain, with the return of the Conservatives to power in 1970, the Government again brought forward the Labour plan for regulating the right to strike – and the Industrial Relations Act was passed in 1971. Immunity was accorded to strikers only in strikes officially called by properly registered unions; in the case of strikes that would threaten the national interest, a cooling-off period and voting by secret ballot could be enforced; go-slows, work-to-rules and overtime bans were all made potentially illegal. In fact, the law was scarcely applied at all, and the return of Labour in 1974 saw its repeal.

In other countries the right to strike was no more strictly regulated after the period of fierce conflict, but the courts were readier to condemn, and employers to penalize (by dismissal), anyone found to be fomenting radical actions.

Repression, then, is generally no more than a palliative; the ruling class is aware that of itself it will not produce the hoped-for formalization. It serves as a preventive, a safety-rail that can be used as a last resort if all other means of formalization fail. But there *are* a great many others: they involve the various levels of negotiation, but they also involve an attempt to give joint consultative machinery a greater role in the system of labour relations. The campaign to formalize takes place on all fronts. But it is strongest at the level of the workplace, since that has been the weakest point in the system – it is at that level that we find most efforts to sabotage it.

There are various changes to indicate advancing formalization at company level. The workplace becomes the scene of major negotiations; firms come more and more to recognize the union as such; the traditional structures for cooperation (works council, works committee, etc.) fulfil more functions than they did before. Thus the aim is to formalize industrial disputes by setting up negotiating structures from which no subject is excluded *a priori*; each side respects the other's right to speak. In France, since the end of 1968, the law has formalized the presence of the union organization in the workplace, but has not always explicitly allowed it a role in negotiations at that level. The functions of *comités d'entreprise* have been extended continually (job-supervision, keeping a check on the work done by women and young people, on working conditions, on in-work training schemes and so on). Since 1968 it has become more usual for companies to sign agreements which make specific reference to national agreements or trade agreements. However, the right of workers to hold meetings on the premises during working hours is still recognized in only a small proportion of firms.

In Italy the position of the union organization in the workplace has continued to improve since 1969: delegates' councils have come to be recognized in all collective agreements, and more and more of the delegates have joined unions; company agreements have begun to embody clauses relating to conditions of work; it has become normal to consult the rank and file before formulating programmes of demands; labour legislation recognizes the right of assembly. There even seems to be a suggestion of ensuring the formalization of industrial relations at top level: in February 1973 the secretary general of the CGIL spoke in favour of a unilateral declaration by the unions that they would undertake not to make new industrial demands between agreements, and would repress sectoral pressures from particular trades.

In Belgium, after the economic and social conference held in March 1970, there were several agreements which strengthened the role of workers' representative structures within their firms: works councils must be consulted over general economic prospects, job development, and the problems of training, re-training and the reorganization of work; they must be given written information on all these points; when they make a recommendation, they must receive a response to it. Parallel to this, the role of trade union representatives has been strengthened: union representatives – of whom there are now more, and whose training is subsidized – can in future keep in touch with workers in their workplace and during working hours; they can also negotiate agreements with particular firms.

In Germany regulations have been made to reinforce the powers of works councils, and also the rights of trade union officers on the shop floor. Naturally the coming to power of the SPD in 1969 and its remaining there in 1972 made legislation of this kind much easier to put through, though its alliance with the Liberal Party has prevented the spread of one reform – that of workers' co-determination.

Great Britain is certainly the place where formalization has made the least progress at company and factory level since the wave of strikes of 1969 and 1970. The main reason was undoubtedly the return of the Conservatives to power in 1970. As we have seen, they resurrected the bill which sought to regulate industrial disputes from above by the establishment of new mechanisms and special tribunals, and by restricting the right to call wildcat strikes. With the return of Labour, formalization began to make some progress, in various directions. The first, and most important for the British economy, was the system of top-level tripartite wage negotiations – the 'Social Contract'. By it the unions accepted a sharp restriction of wage increases. The second sign of increasing formalization was the coming into force of the Employment Protection Act early in 1976. This law set up, or reinforced, machinery for conciliation and arbitration, and extended the rights of the unions at every level: unions were entitled to nominate representatives to health and safety committees; union officers were protected against unfair dismissal and were given the right to time off with pay for union activities; the law required employers to disclose to union representatives information required for collective bargaining purposes; and many benefits were restricted to unions certified to be independent of the employer. Additionally, women were given an entitlement to six weeks' maternity pay.

The third major change is still under discussion: at the end of 1976 the Bullock Committee on Industrial Democracy was considering the possibility of bringing workers' representatives onto the management boards of companies; if this were to happen it would start the machinery for joint consultation going again and extend formalization at company and factory level. There were four reasons for undertaking such a discussion: to give more concrete shape to the Labour Party programme for nationalization, to reduce industrial conflict, to increase productivity and to give workers greater job satisfaction (Loveridge, 1976).

The fourth area in which it looks as though formalization will be increased is also at company level: the improvement of working conditions. In December 1974 the government announced the setting up of a Work Research Unit at the Ministry of Labour; in mid-1975 it published a report, *Making Work More Satisfying;* it promised to start discussions with company managements aimed at (a) making work use fully the skills and capacities of the individual, (b) providing opportunities for learning and personal development, (c) giving the worker greater responsibility, (d) giving scope for more contact with fellow-workers, and so on. This might also start up joint consultation procedures again. The aim in view is to try and achieve a consensus between the two sides – for without that there can be no effective formalization.

In every country, then, the first waves of strikes created the objective conditions for extending the formalization of industrial disputes; they also resulted in to some extent remedying the earlier weaknesses in the system of industrial relations on the shop floor. Paradoxically, they also produced the objective conditions for more radical action and a further spread of sabotage: the reinforcement of procedures for formalizing disputes also contained the seeds of its own negation. So, just at the point when the problem of updating the formalizing of disputes on the shopfloor began to be resolved, its very foundations were brought into doubt.

The radicalization of disputes in the period following the first waves of strikes is evident from the fact that workers began turning more readily to various forms of sabotage (indefinite strikes, concerted disorganization of production, factory occupations, direct actions, taking over control of production). This radicalization can be explained partly by the advances in formalization: instead of being directed to getting rid of weaknesses in the system, disputes were now seeking to bring into question the industrial peace which that formalization seemed to imply.

'Intelligent' formalization can in fact be turned against itself: if the union organization is recognized as having a voice on the shopfloor, then indirectly this enables the workers to organize better in disputes, without any fear of immediate repression. Similarly, the negotiation of demands which had hitherto been considered non-negotiable (working conditions, for instance) can, if talks break down, easily lead to the workers resorting to direct action. The apparent increase in the power of consultative bodies (works councils or committees) soon results in a realization of their constitutional weakness – having a whole lot more powers of consultation and theoretical control still does not make the vital difference of giving them actual powers of decision (even in Germany, where the system is most advanced, workers' co-determination is not as egalitarian as it appears). On the supervisory boards of mines and steelworks, the 'eleventh man' chosen by both sides is far more likely to side with the management. Strengthening the consultative role of such structures is all too likely to appear illusory very soon. Recognition of the illusion can lead to demands for real power, but it can also lead to a radicalization of disputes which then becomes part of a wider aim to change society – the only effective way to overthrow the power of the ruling class.

The radicalization of forms of struggle does not rest only on recent modifications in the formalization of industrial disputes. It permits a radicalization of ideology – which also justifies it. Obviously there are degrees of ideological radicalization: though all these ideologies admit the need to change society and achieve socialism or communism, there are disagreements over the way such a change should take place, whether by revolution or via the ballot box. Radical ideologies are supported mainly by student groups but also by some sectors of the workers' movement. In all these countries – alongside the more or less steady process of trade union amalgamation (around immediate demands or longer-term social aims) – there has been a move to the Left. Thus within the amalgamated unions there will be some federations which take an explicitly leftist stand: this is true of the metal workers' unions in Britain, Germany and Italy, and also of transport workers and miners in Britain. In France the CGT gave unequivocal support to the general platform of the Left in the electoral campaigns of 1973 and 1974; the CFDT became associated with this in 1974. More significantly, at its 1970 congress its statutes were so framed as to embody a commitment to the class struggle and an intention to work for a socialist society based upon three interconnected foundations – the social ownership of the means of production, workers' self-management and democratic planning. In Belgium, too, the Socialist union federation, the FGTB, hardened its attitude over workers' control at its 1971 congress. This general radicalizing of trade union ideologies was certainly a consequence of the strikes of 1968–70, but it also represents a new frame of reference, a starting-point for radicalizing the tactics of struggle.

The first waves of strikes, then, which arose because industrial relations were insufficiently formalized, resulted on the one hand in radicalizing later disputes, and on the other in increasing formalization at company level – which contained in itself the seeds of its negation and thus contributed to a further intensification of the radicalizing process. The management move to prevent sabotage by bringing all negotiation into the context of the trade unions is thus not invariably successful.

The ideology of growth

Confronted with sabotage activities by workers, all aimed at lowering production, managements wage an ideological campaign to bring home the advantages of boosting production: in the early fifties there was the mirage of productivity; in the sixties they offered participation and profit-sharing schemes as an incentive to expansion; in the seventies stress has been laid on the virtues of 'growth'. The underlying reasoning is the same in each case: only with sustained expansion, a continuing increase in productivity, can the national income be painlessly redistributed to benefit the workers. Alas, no such redistribution has occurred to any significant extent in the past thirty years. Yet the unions have succumbed, and are indeed still succumbing, to the temptation of signing agreements based on the assumption that it will. After the Second World War the United States stood supreme: they wanted to assist the recovery of Europe by helping it with large financial subsidies – the Marshall Plan. The C G T were hostile to American aid but they were by no means hostile to adopting American methods to foster increased productivity. The word was on everyone's lips; so-called 'productivity study groups' were sent to the U S to learn from their example. In 1951 the three French union federations – the C G T, C F T C and F O – decided to set up an inter-union Centre of Study and Research for Production. That same year the two sides in the textile industry introduced productivity into a completely new national collective agreement: 'The undersigned organizations recognize the advantage of improving productivity in their industry, insofar as it will improve the quantity and quality of products available to customers, reduce prices, increase the purchasing power of wages and improve working conditions.' The unions therefore put up no opposition to the automation of plant or the reorganization of work methods. The prevailing spirit was one of what was then called in France *paritarisme* (worker/management collaboration on a parity basis). 1955 was the year of the famous Renault agreement: the management tried to make the unions recognize that 'the experience of the past few years has shown that, in a favourable economic situation, the normal functioning of the Renault factories, characterized by a permanent atmosphere of industrial peace, has produced such prosperity that the standard of living of all the employees has risen gradually but significantly'. Workers' conditions improve if production goes up; production will go up if there is industrial peace; *ergo*, do nothing to interfere with production, and the future will be rosy.

In the sixties the campaign was mounted more intensively

still, with the introduction of the ideology of workers' participation and the linking of wages to profits. Committees met and argued. Workers must be made to understand that it was not in their interest to adopt restrictive practices since, by the new arrangement whereby employees would share in the benefits of expansion, they themselves would be the first to suffer. 'It seems that from now on we are entering a new phase in improving the condition of wage-earners: workers must participate in the growth of their firms, and benefit directly from it ... Progress, which all help to effect, must be a source of enrichment to all; in other words, everyone must have some share in the increased capital that results from it.' As well as profit-sharing, there were also experiments in making workers shareholders in the public sector, starting with Renault and then in banking and insurance.

Private employers were as insistent as public authorities on the indispensability of growth. At an industrial management conference in Marseilles in October 1972 it was the central theme in the discussions: industry, growth, and people. The report on growth and society began with this sentence: 'Growth is the prerequisite of social progress: financing growth means financing social progress.' But growth results not from capital investment alone, but also from human hard work. The conference looked at the question of how to change working conditions to encourage harder work – so that people could be rewarded for making greater efforts.

It is fine for employers to have this ideology of growth in a period of expansion. But what comes of it when, as in 1975, industrial production shows a negative growth rate? The workers are still determined to improve their situation; realizing that they will not do so by making a great all-out effort to work, since there will be no buyer for their product, they may well decide on sabotage of various kinds combined with demanding a greater share of the existing cake.

The great ideological campaign by employers and governments to bring home to the workers the equations: 'Economic growth= social progress' and 'Economic growth = worker effort + productive investment', has never yet managed to put a stop to sabotage, to the tendency for workers to expend the minimum effort. But that deters no one. Each campaign is short-lived, and it starts up again a few months later, trying to convey the same message in different words. The object is achieved if the workers become imbued with a productive spirit and start thinking in terms of 'respect for the machinery of production', 'effort', 'self-sacrifice', 'we're not in this just for fun' (i.e., being proud of killing oneself on the job), 'doing one's best', 'the satisfaction of having got there by one's own efforts'. Indeed, the ideological attack can only be successful in getting rid of sabotage if it is waged conjointly by management and the workers' representatives; the formalization of industrial relations is then complete. But, as we have seen, this has very little chance of achieving the desired result.

Summary

The responses of employers to worker sabotage can be very various. In the last century it was most likely to take the form of authoritarianism, with violent, disciplinary and penal repression. The workers no longer owned the means of production, but they still had control of their own work organization, and therefore still had considerable scope for sabotaging both machinery and products – by going slow, striking or staying off work. They knew they could not easily be replaced.

Mass production led to a change in the distribution of jobs and a need for less skill in the workforce. It therefore enabled the employers to break the power of skilled craftsmen. This was the first and very effective response of the employers to worker sabotage. But because the new methods also involved setting up larger factories and ceasing to recognize workers' representative organizations, they failed to achieve the employers' objective: the anonymity of large work units also provided anonymity for acts of sabotage.

It is during our own period that the employers' response seems to have become most effective and varied. There is still an apparatus of repression available: it is used very little, but an outcrop of sabotage will be met by recourse to more punitive legislation, at least for a short time. Generally, however, gentler methods are preferred: more flexible systems of management, job-enlargement, setting up autonomous production groups, recognizing trade union organizations even in the workplace, formalizing negotiating methods, building smaller factories, promoting the ideology of growth. We find such management manoeuvres to counter sabotage in many different places. They do not remove the risk, however. All such responses tend to give the workers back some power – apparent or real – over the way their work is organized. And, as studies have shown, workers who have been given autonomy in their jobs become attached to it. Autonomy breeds autonomy. Once workers begin to regain the power to organize their own work, what then? Surely they will one day say, 'We want it all' – including the means of production. 'We don't want more bread. We want the bakery!'

Conclusion

I have tried in this book to explain why workers sometimes resort to sabotage – in which I include damaging machinery and products, arson and theft, indefinite strikes (supported by blacking), going slow, working to rule, absenteeism, labour turnover, avoiding employment or just refusing to enter industry at all. There can obviously be many reasons for it: the satisfaction of an immediate demand, setting in motion a revolutionary process, simply expressing their antagonism to the management, getting their own back when a strike has failed, despair of gaining what they want by other means, or a response to repressive measures on the part of the employers. The nature of the work, the industrial experience of the workers, the amount of power wielded by the unions, management policy, how well the negotiating system works, the history of disputes in the firm concerned, repressive legislation, prevailing theories, and ideas held by minorities – all these factors may help in one way or another to explain the appearance of sabotage in various places, and its resurgence at the present time. It is hard to assess their relative importance. One can, however, contrast two types of situation: where the work is unskilled, where there is no industrial or trade union tradition, where management is authoritarian, and where the negotiating system breaks down – where the risks of an outbreak of certain sorts of sabotage are very great; on the other hand, new forms of work organization giving workers more responsibility, the establishment of strong union organizations and a permanent and effective negotiating system – where the risks of sabotage are generally reduced. But the mere fact of a number of such factors coexisting can never wholly remove all risk. Sabotage, in its various forms, will always remain a possible expedient for the workers' movement – if only of a minority – as long as the vital problem of the ownership of the means of production is left unresolved. So we find ourselves back at the point where we started. Surely the reason a worker turns to sabotage is because he says to himself: 'These machines aren't mine, this product isn't mine, this way of organizing work isn't mine, these production targets (both quantity and quality) have been set by someone else. There's nothing in it for me.'

Can we forecast how patterns of sabotage will develop in the future? Not with any certainty, of course. For instance, let us look only at the effect of one factor of which I have said little so far: the economic situation. At a time when there is unemployment in all the economies of the west, what happens to sabotage? History shows that violent methods, including the destruction of machinery and products, have sometimes been used to counter redundancies. The modern form of this tactic is the campaign tried out at the Lip works, and the sort of thing they did there seems likely to become more widespread (going slow, expropriating the finished product, dismantling machinery, all-out strikes). Theft will also probably mount: this the worker will justify by saying that he is squaring accounts with the boss before he goes. Long strikes to save jobs may increase – the Lip strike in 1973 lasted eight months; the strike in the Annonay tanneries lasted thirteen, ending in July 1975. Going slow is a normal response when workers feel their jobs threatened: the work will last longer if production is drawn out. There may be an overall trend towards working without enthusiasm, though individuals may well try to produce better-quality work than before in the hope of not being among the first to lose their jobs. Avoidance of employment may become a more attractive option for some people, especially now that it has become financially profitable; a French agreement of 14 October 1974 stipulates that workers made redundant for economic reasons should be paid 90 per cent of their wages for a year. Not everyone is tempted to take a sabbatical of this kind, but it seems likely that more and more will do so if underemployment should become established as not just a temporary phenomenon but a regular state of things. Unlike the forms of sabotage I have just mentioned (which unemployment will probably contribute to increasing) there are others that are liable to disappear when work is hard to get: labour turnover goes down in times of recession (people do not move about when the available jobs are limited); absenteeism also goes down (as statistical studies have shown) – the boss must be given no excuse for making *me* one of the first to be laid off – though this attitude may alter as unemployment pay becomes more attractive. Finally, the resistance to going into industry should also be overcome by rising unemployment: one is not so fussy about the kind of job one takes when there are millions out of work – though here too a high rate of unemployment pay may alter the picture. Paid non-work may be more appealing than a job that is merely boring and exhausting drudgery. All in all, then, we may say that unemployment is more likely to favour sabotage than not.

Are we forced to conclude that *nothing* will ever get rid of worker sabotage? I myself believe that all the factors we have looked at in this study contribute to the more or less widespread existence of sabotage; but, fundamentally, that sabotage as such is bound up with the private ownership of the means of production, and will disappear only when that does. But a change of *ownership* is not all that is needed: the workers must also regain control of the *organization* of their own work and the *ends* for which they are producing. In other words, the social ownership of the means of production must be accompanied by democratic planning and workers' self-management. When economic development is based on the satisfaction of human needs, when the social division of labour has disappeared, when social relations are egalitarian rather than hierarchical, when there is a fairer distribution of incomes, when the workers participate democratically in determining the aims of production and the organization of their work – when we have finally achieved socialism with freedom, in other words – then sabotage will cease.

Bibliography

Andréani, E. (1968), *Grèves et fluctuations: La France de 1890 à 1914*, Cujas, Paris.

Arendt, H. (1972), *Crises of the Republic*, Penguin.

Argyle, M., G. Gardner and F. Cioffi (1965), 'Supervisory methods related to productivity, absenteeism and turnover', in Turner and Lawrence (1965).

Arnison, J. (1970), *The Million Pound Strike*, Lawrence & Wishart.

Barou, J. P. (1975), *Gilda, je t'aime! A bas le travail!*, Les Presses d'aujourd'hui, Paris.

Barrier, C. (1975), *Le Combat ouvrier dans une entreprise de pointe*, Les Éditions ouvrières, Paris.

Becker, J. J. (1973), *Le Carnet B.*, Éditions Klincksieck, Paris.

Behrend, H., and S. Pocock (1976), 'L'absentéisme individuel', *Revue internationale du travail*, vol. 114, no. 3, November–December, 345–63.

Benoist, L. (1970), *Le Compagnonnage et les métiers*, Que sais-je?, Paris.

Bergerie (1829–30), *Économie industrielle*, Paris.

Bernoux, P., D. Motte and J. Saglio (1973), *Trois ateliers d'O.S.*, Les Éditions ouvrières, Paris.

Blondeau, Y. (1973), *Le Syndicat des correcteurs*, Éditions Syndicat des correcteurs, Paris.

Bourdet, Y. (1970), *La Délivrance de Prométhée*, Anthropos, Paris.

Bourdet, Y. (1974), *Pour l'autogestion*, Anthropos, Paris.

Brecher, J. (1972), *Strike!*, Straight Arrow, San Francisco.

Brecy, P. (1969), *La Grève générale en France*, EDI, Paris.

Briggs, A. (1965), *Victorian People*, Penguin.

Brown, W. (1973), *Piecework Bargaining*, Heinemann Educational.

Brunhes, D. (1974), 'Les progrès de productivité du travail depuis vingt-cinq ans', INSEE, *Économie et Statistique*, 62, December, 27–42.

Cazamian, P. (1974), 'L'Ergonomie industrielle', *Après demain*, January, 34ff.

Chamberlain, N., and J. Metzger Schilling (1954), *The Impact of Strikes, Their Social and Economic Costs*, Harper, New York.

Clegg, H. A. (1972), *The System of Industrial Relations in Great Britain*, Basil Blackwell, Oxford.

Dassa, S., J. Y. Fournier and N. Mercier (1973), *Les Relations professionnelles dans l'entreprise*, Laboratoire de Sociologie du Travail et des Relations professionnelles, Paris.

Denis, H. (1963), *Le Comité parisien de la Libération*, P U F, Paris.

Dijkstra, A. (1974), 'La réduction du personnel des entreprises et l'absentéisme pour maladie', *Sociologische Gids* (Netherlands), 21, No. 1, 3–15.

Dommanget, M. (1972), *Histoire du Premier Mai*, Éditions de la Tête de Feuille, Paris.

Donovan, Lord (1971), *Royal Commission on Trade Unions and Employers' Associations*, H M S O.

Dubois, P. (1973), 'Comment transformer les conditions de travail?', *Économie et humanisme*, 214, November–December, 27–45.

Dubois, P. (1974a), *Formes de luttes dans les usines nouvelles*, Groupe de Sociologie du Travail, Paris.

Dubois, P. (1974b), *Les Nouvelles Formes des conflits du travail en Europe*, Groupe de Sociologie du Travail, Paris.

Dubois, P. (1974c), 'Les grèves et le droit à l'emploi', *Revue française des affaires sociales*, January–March, 119–53.

Dubois, P., and C. Durand (1975), *La Grève*, Armand Colin, Paris.

Dubois, P., R. Dulong, C. Durand, S. Erbes-Séguin and D. Vidal (1971), *Grèves revendicatives ou grèves politiques?*, Anthropos, Paris.

Dumont, J. P. (1972), 'Attitudes des ouvriers à l'égard du travail en usine. Travail contesté ou travail saboté', paper given to a seminar of the Association française de science politique, Paris, 3 and 4 November.

Durand, C., C. Prestat and A. Willener (1972), *Travail, salaire, production. I: Le contrôle des cadences*, Mouton, Paris.

Durand, M., and Y. Harff (1973), 'Panorama statistique des grèves', *Sociologie du travail*, 4, 356–75.

Durand, R. (1971), *La Lutte des travailleurs de chez Renault racontée par eux-mêmes*, Éditions sociales, Souvenirs, Paris.

Engels, F. (1845), *The Condition of the Working-Class in England in 1844*, first published in English in 1892; reissued by Basil Blackwell, Oxford, 1971.

Faye, J.-P. (1973), *Lutte de classes à Dunkerque*, Éditions Galilée, Paris.

Fisher, M. (1973), *Mesure des conflits du travail et de leurs répercussions économiques*, OCDE, Paris.

Fohlen, C. (1972), *Le Travail au XIXe siècle*, Que sais-je?, Paris.

Frischmann, G. (1967), *Histoire de la fédération CGT des PTT*, Éditions sociales, Paris.

Frow, R. and E., and M. Katanka (1971), *Strikes: A Documentary History*, Charles Knight, London.

Goetz-Girey, R. (1965), *Le Mouvement des grèves en France*, Sirey, Paris.

Guérin, D. (1968), *Le Mouvement ouvrier aux États-Unis, 1867–1967*, Maspero, Paris.

Hacker, F. (1972), *Aggression et violence dans le monde moderne*, Calmann-Lévy, Paris.

Hameed, S. M. A., and T. Lomas (1975), 'Measurement of production losses due to strikes in Canada: an input-output analysis', *British Journal of Industrial Relations*, XIII, no. 1, March, 86–93.

Hess, R. (1974), *Les Maoïstes français, une dérive institutionelle*, Anthropos, Paris.

Hethy, L., and C. Mako (1971), 'La rémunération au rendement dans une entreprise hongroise', *Sociologie du travail*, I, 25–37.

Hethy, L., and C. Mako (1974), 'Work performance, interests, powers and environment. The case of cyclical slowdowns in a Hungarian factory', *European Economic Review*, 5, 141–57.

Hill, J. M. M., and E. L. Trist (1955), 'Changes in accidents and other absences with length of service', *Human Relations*, 8, 121–52.

Hobsbawm, E. J. (1964), *Labouring Men*, Weidenfeld & Nicolson.

Hyman, R. (1972), *Strikes*, Fontana.

Jacquet, J. (1967), *Les Cheminots dans l'histoire sociale de France*, Fédération nationale des cheminots CGT, Éditions sociales, Paris.

Jardillier, P. (1962), 'Étude de 14 facteurs influant sur l'absentéisme industriel', *Le Travail humain*, 25th year, nos. 1–2.

Karsh, B. (1958), *Diary of a Strike*, University of Illinois Press.

Kessel, P. (1972), *Le Mouvement maoïste en France*, vol. 1, UGE, Paris.

Knowles, J. (1954) *Strikes: A Study in Industrial Conflict*, Blackwell, Oxford.

Lefranc, G. (1967), *Le Mouvement syndical sous la Troisième République*, Payot, Paris.

Lefranc, G. (1969), *Le Mouvement syndical de la Libération aux événements de mai-juin 1968*, Payot, Paris.

Lévy, C. (1974), *La Libération*, PUF, Paris.

L'Huillier, F. (1958), *La Lutte ouvrière à la fin du Second Empire*, Armand Colin, Paris.

Lourau, R. (1974), *L'Analyseur Lip*, UGE, Paris.

Loveridge, R. A. (1976), unpublished paper.

Lupton, T. (1963), *On the Shop Floor: Two Studies of Workshop Organisation*, Pergamon, Oxford.

Lyons, T. F. (1972), 'Turnover and absenteeism: A review of relationships and shared correlates', *Personnel Psychology*, 25, 271–81.

Maitron, J. (1975), *Le Mouvement anarchiste en France. I: Des origines à 1914*, Maspero, Paris.

Mallet, S. (1970), *L'Après-mai 1968*, *grèves pour le contrôle ouvrier*, paper delivered to a meeting of the Arbresle, Lyon, December.

Manceau, H. (1969), *Des luttes ardennaises*, Éditions sociales, Paris.

Mellor, W. (1920), *Direct Action*, Parsons.

McCarthy, W.E.J. (1969), 'Shop stewards' bargaining in Britain', in A. Flanders (ed.), *Collective Bargaining*, Penguin.

Michaud, R. (1967), *J'avais vingt ans. Un jeune homme du début du siècle*, Éditions syndicalistes, Paris.

Moissonnier, M. (1975), *La Révolte des canuts*, Éditions sociales, Paris.

Mottez, B. (1971), *La Sociologie industrielle*, Que sais-je?, Paris.

Moussy, J.-P., et al. (1974), *Le Mai des banques*, Syros, Paris.

Nicholson, N. (1976), 'Management sanctions and absence control', *Human Relations*, vol. 29, no. 2, 139–51.

Nieburg, H. L. (1963), 'Uses of violence', *Journal of Conflict Resolution*, VII, no. 1, March, 44–6.

Pelling, H. (1963), *A History of British Trade Unionism*, Penguin.

Perdu, J. (1974), *La Révolte des canuts, 1831–1834*, Spartacus, Paris.

Perrot, M. (1973), *Les Ouvriers en grève. France, 1871–1890*, Mouton, Paris.

Piaget, G. (1973), *Lip*, Stock, Paris.

Pierre, R. (1973), *Les Origines du syndicalisme et du socialisme dans la Drôme*, Éditions sociales, Paris.

Platania, F. (1974), 'Vingt-trois années chez Fiat', *Les Temps modernes*, no. 335, June, 2286–2302.

Pouget, E. (1910), *Le Sabotage*, reissued by Graphedis, Paris, 1969.

Pouget, E., and R. Pataud (1911), *Comment nous ferons la révolution!*, Éditions de la guerre sociale, Paris.

Ratgeb (1974), *De la grève sauvage à l'autogestion généralisée*, UGE, Paris.

Rolle, P. (1962), 'Normes et chronométrage dans le salaire au rendement', *Cahiers d'étude de l'automation et des sociétés industrielles*, 4, 9–38.

Rosow, J. M. (1974), *The Worker and the Job*, Prentice Hall, Engle-wood Cliffs, N.J.

Ross, J. C., and *A. Zander* (1964), 'Need satisfaction and employee turnover', in V. H. Vroom, *Work and Motivation*, Wiley, New York.

Rousselet, J. (1974), *L'Allergie au travail*, Le Seuil, Paris.

Saglio, A., and *M. Tabuteau* (1971), 'L'utilisation des capacités de pro-duction dans l'industrie', INSEE, *Économie et statistique*, 21, March, 13–32.

Sartin, P. (1970), *L'Homme au travail, forçat du temps?*, Gamma, Paris.

Sartori, G. (1972), 'Le pouvoir des syndicats ouvriers dans la société technocratique. Une analyse prospective', paper given to a seminar of the Association française de science politique, Paris, 3 and 4 November.

Scardigli, V. (1974), *Les Grèves dans l'économie française*, CREDOC, Paris.

Shorter, E. L., and *C. Tilly* (1971), 'Le déclin de la grève violente en France de 1890 à 1935', *Le Mouvement social*, no. 76, July–September, 95–118.

Shorter, E. L., and *C. Tilly* (1973), 'Les vagues de grèves en France, 1890–1968', *Les Annales*, 4, July–August, 857–87.

Sorel, G. (1908), *Réflections sur la violence*, republished in English as *Reflections on Violence*, AMS Press, New York, 1975.

Taylor, F. W. (1909), *Scientific Management*, reissued by Greenwood Press, Westport, Conn., 1972.

Taylor, L., and *P. Walton* (1971), 'Industrial sabotage: Motives and meanings', in S. Cohen, *Images of Deviance*, Penguin.

Thompson, E. P. (1963), *The Making of the English Working Class*, Victor Gollancz; revised edition, Penguin, 1968.

Turner, A. N., and *P. R. Lawrence* (1965), *Industrial Jobs and the Worker*, Harvard Business School, Boston.

Union des industries métallurgiques et minières (n.d.), *L'Absentéisme en 1971 dans les industries des métaux*, Liaisons sociales, Documents 12/73.

Virieu, F. H. de (1973), *Lip. 100,000 montres sans patron*, Calmann-Lévy, Paris.

Wilson, D. E. (1972), *Dockers, The Impact of Social Change*, Fontana.

Wisner, A., A. Laville, C. Teiger and *J. Duraffourg* (1972), *Conséquences du travail répétitif sous cadence sur la santé des travailleurs et les accidents*, CNAM, Paris, Laboratoire de physiologie du travail et d'ergonomie, no. 29, March.

XXX (1973), 'Le mouvement des OS de Renault Flins', *Les Temps modernes*, no. 323, 2163–2241.

Index